CO

Reading Pictures,
Viewing Texts

READING PICTURES, VIEWING TEXTS

CLAUDE GANDELMAN

INDIANA UNIVERSITY PRESS

Bloomington and Indianapolis

Earlier versions of chaps. I, II, VII, and XI were published in
Claude Gandelman, *Le regard dans le texte: Peinture et écriture
du quattrocento au XXe siècle* (Paris: Méridiens-Klincksieck,
1986). Chap. III is based on an article that appeared in *Versus*, no. 37
(Jan.–Apr. 1984), pp. 55–70 (Bologna University). Chap. VII is based on an article
that appeared
in *Littérature*, no. 53 (Feb. 1984), pp. 3–17 (Paris, Larousse).

The paper used in this publication meets the minimum requirements of American
National Standard for Information Sciences—Permanence of Paper for Printed
Library Materials, ANSI Z39.48-1984.

Manufactured in the United States of America

Library of Congress Cataloging-in-Publication Data

Gandelman, Claude.
Reading pictures, viewing texts / Claude Gandelman.
p.   cm.
Includes index
ISBN 0-253-32532-3 (alk. paper)
1. Arts—Psychological aspects. 2. Arts—Philosophy.
3. Apperception. 4. Art—Appreciation. I. Title.
NX175.G36   1990
700'.1—dc20   90-42147
CIP

1 2 3 4 5 94 93 92 91

CONTENTS

To Richard Exner and Naomi Greene,
whose friendship made the completion of this book possible

ACKNOWLEDGMENTS

I would like to thank the following artists, poets, and scholars who graciously gave me permission to reproduce works belonging to them or to their estates: Arnold Belkin, Mexico City; Max Bense, Stuttgart; Anne-Marie Gillion-Crowet, Brussels; Adolfo Hernandez Diaz and the Brothers of Santa Caridad in Seville; Helmut Heissenbüttel, Borsfleth; Tim Ulrich, Hannover; Marian Stauffer and the University Press of Delaware, Newark; M. Guillaume, Curator of the Dijon Museum; B. T. Galloway of the National Gallery, London; Warren Kenton, alias Ze'ev Ben Shimon Halevy, a London cabalist; Georgia Prince and Plenum Publishing Corporation; Professor Alfred L. Yarbus, Moscow; Arlena W. Sullivan and the Johns Hopkins University Press, Baltimore; Díaz Canedo and the Joaquín Mortiz Publishing House; Cécile Talamon, Méridiens-Klincksieck, Paris; Jacques Neefs, *Littérature*, Paris; Umberto Eco, Bologna; I. A. M. Wilke, State Museum for Prussian Culture, West Berlin; and Serge Lemoine, Chief Curator, and Isabelle Varloteaux, Documentalist, Grenoble Museum.

Special thanks to my good friends in Mexico, Adriana de Vries and Elizabeth Siefer, who made special efforts to get me the necessary permissions, and to Dr. Ephraim Sicher, Ben Gurion University, an Isaac Babel scholar who provided me with invaluable information, and Thomas D. Grischovsky, Museum of Modern Art, New York, who helped me locate the copyright owner of a picture seldom reproduced.

INTRODUCTION

At the beginning of a conference not long ago on primitive art and communication chaired by Claude Lévi-Strauss, in which I had the honor of participating, the great anthropologist said that, as he saw it, the conference should be placed under the aegis of Alois Riegl, who was the first to attempt writing both a grammar of visual forms and a grammar of our apperception of these forms. As it turned out, the conference went its own way, as conferences will do, without much heeding the advice of its chairman. As far as I was concerned, however, the advice was well taken. I had already written peripherally on Riegl, particularly concerning the influence of his *Spaetromanische Kunstindustrie* on Weimar aesthetics, and was convinced that Riegl's formalistic, or grammatical, approach to the visual arts could still yield discoveries in both the visual and the textual fields.

I have therefore placed this book—as Lévi-Strauss recommended for the conference—under the aegis of Alois Riegl and his great dichotomy, the *optic* and the *haptic*. One reads a picture either haptically (by touch, visual touch) or optically (according to the pure vectoriality of outlines), or by a dialectical combining of the two visions. And this book is about reading. Not just the reading of texts but also—insofar as it is legitimate to extend the metaphor—the reading of pictures.

This book is also about the relationship between the visual and the textual and sometimes about the equivalence of the visual and the verbal. That is especially the case in the penultimate chapter, XI, which deals with the phenomenon of concrete poetry of the past decade. Chapter II, in a way, also deals with the verbal content of a common human gesture, the gesture of showing with the pointed finger. For whom, for what type of observer, does a represented character "show"? And what does showing mean in the context of the visual arts and literature?

Doors, or at least doors as signs in paintings and pictures, may also be equated with a sort of pointing gesture. Doors motion us to enter the space of the representation. Yet doors are also what the Latin tongue called *limina*, thresholds. As such, they are indeed liminal, devices in a sort of passage rite accomplished by our regard, by our reading. Chapter III deals at length with this analogy, a phenomenon that has been studied primarily by anthropology.

Artists produce horrifying images of the body, sometimes of their own bodies. One such artist is Kafka, who saw himself and the artist in general as a "hunger artist." In chapter IV I have tried to place the skeletonlike artist as depicted by Kafka within the general context of his times, of what I call expressionist anorexia. I try, further, to relate this linear image to the linearity and vectoriality of the expressionist narrative.

In chapters VI and VII texts are brought into confrontation with maps. There are texts which contain maps and are read as maps and there are maps which are texts and are read as texts. There are also maps which have the shape of a human head or a human body. Perhaps reading texts is similar to reading a giant portrait. Jorge Luis Borges made that the theme of "Epilogue," one of his short stories: "A man sets about the task of sketching the world. As years go by, he peoples an imaginary space with pictures, provinces, kingdoms, mountains, bays, ships, islands, fish, rooms, instruments, planets, horses and men. A little before he dies, he discovers that this patient labyrinth of lines delineated the picture of his own face." It may indeed happen that a writer discovers his face emerging from his texts like a map, like a landscape. And perhaps, when that happens, it is the sign that he has read everything within himself and seen everything—above all, seen the impossible coming together as one unique entity of verbality and textuality. Is it time for him to die?

Chapters VI through VIII deal also with strange human shapes, the body images all of us bear within ourselves. This is not a poetic metaphor; the chapters were written with reference to the so-called cortical homunculus discovered by physiological science, the implicit image of oneself that a person has inscribed as a sort of imprint in the cortex. Does one also read this image? And what type of reading is this? And does this image not direct the image of the body that emerges in cartoons? Might not caricatures, political or otherwise, be considered a sort of exposition and revelation of the political homunculus within us?

Thus we haptically delve into our own selves and extract our own images, sometimes violently. An extreme case of such a violent reading is the image of the artist's body as Marsyas, the Dionysian demigod flayed by Apollo. Chapters IX and X survey the evolution of the Marsyas myth from ancient Greece to the present.

Concerning the disposition of chapters, I must observe that since the main approach is synchronic rather than diachronic, it was impossible to adhere to a strictly historical chronology. Still, I have tried to present my chapters in some sort of historical order. The one dealing with Renaissance painting, for example, precedes the one dealing with doors because the corpus of doors I investigated extends well into the seventeenth century. And in the haptic section, the chapter dealing with the scatological imagery of the French Revolution precedes the one dealing with the image of the flayed body, which, though it begins with the ancient Marsyas myth, extends deep into the twentieth century.

In the main, the book tends to avoid ideology and theorizing. It is about the apperception of texts and pictures, not about "ways of reading" or "ways of looking" in the sense in which John Berger, inspired by Walter Benjamin, intended those phrases. I am, of course, fully aware that there is no such thing as naive, or virginal, apperception. Riegl, as well as Wittgenstein, murdered the concept of the "innocent eye" of apperception. Psycho-analysis, especially the trend represented by Lacan—see chapter XII—did, too: "Lacan doth murder eye, the innocent eye. . . ." It is the vision of our inner eye which should be privileged as an object of research, not the "socially anchored" vision of Benjamin and Berger. It is primarily the innate structure of vision, the inner body vision we have in our cortex, which directs our gaze when we look at things, when we read them, and only secondarily the social categorizations or the political ideologies. There is a discourse of the body, concealed as a watermark is concealed in paper, behind political discourse. Mikhail Bakhtin was, perhaps, the first to reveal that history is primarily a discourse *about* the body. And sometimes, as in revolutionary situations, it is a discourse *of* the disgusting, flatulent body. Body representation directs political discourse.

In some respects this book is cruel, a sort of theater of cruelty, full of terrible pictures. Arthaud's "cruelty" was prefigured in the visual arts, almost from the beginning. This book is, to a large extent, about the martyrdom inflicted on the eye by vision. Indeed, I feel that I have excuses for laying the emphasis upon this *terribilità* of vision. Artistic creation and aesthetic appreciation probably have more to do with tears, sperm, and blood than with rational, controlled thinking. Artistic creation also has much to do with body vision, with the image of the uncontrollable body that is always in the *Hintergrund* of political, historical, and aesthetic discourse. It is the "terribility" of this uncontrollable body that aesthetic sadism means to describe, and perhaps to control.

I

TOUCHING WITH THE EYE

The eye is a tactile creature, an agent of human contact. By virtue of its mere touch, the eye gives life.

In Egypt the self-generated god Ra, the sun-god who begets his own self, is seen as a human eye ☞. Ra may also appear as *âri*, "the maker," and the various hieroglyphic forms of the verb *to do* almost always contain an eye: for example, "it was done" ☞𓂝 . Thus the eye is the symbol par excellence of the performative verb.

Another ancient Egyptian eye is the *wajat*-eye (fig. I.l), the precious left eye of Horus that was stolen by Seth and subsequently restored by Thoth. This eye is often endowed with a human hand, as in a picture painted on the vault of the tomb of Pashedu, a nobleman of the Twentieth Dynasty (fig. I.2). The manifold hands represented as rays emanating from many Egyptian paintings of Ra are similarly well known.

This very hieroglyph, the eye that touches things, may be found in modern form in the gesticulation of Courbet as he paints a model in his studio (fig. I.3). The connection with the hieratic imagery of antiquity was not totally absent from Courbet's thoughts. He mentions his own "Assyrian profile" in a famous programmatic letter to Champfleury concerning *The Painter's Studio*.[1]

The hieroglyph formed by the hand and eye of the painter is a sign of a new doctrine: the militant realism of Courbet touches things with the eye. French nineteenth-century realism was oculocentrist—in a very special sense. For the exponents of this aesthetic current, the ideal was the unmediated capturing of reality, and the eye was the agent par excellence of this sort of touching. It is therefore no wonder that the hieroglyph of the eye that is also a hand should have reemerged in a picture by Courbet.

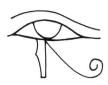

I.1 *Wajat*-eye.

1

I.2 The *Wajat*-eye in the tomb
of Pashedu in Egypt.

The eye–touch concept had several revivals in the trajectory described by
aesthetic developments leading to French realism. One period in which this
idea reemerged was the sixteenth century, with its emphasis on emblematics.
The emblem-making artists of the period were outspoken in asserting that
they were creating veritable hieroglyphs.[2] That may explain why one of the
best-known Renaissance emblems, Julius Wilhelm Zincgref's *Emblematicum*

I.3 *The Painter's Studio* by Gustave
Courbet (detail). Diagram shows
painter's hand and eye.
Photo Museés Nationaux, Paris.

I.4 Emblematic "hieroglyph" from Zincgref's
Emblematicum Ethico-Politorum.
Author's photograph.

Ethico-Politorum, shows an eye inserted into the palm of an open hand, seemingly looking at the world from the palm of this hand (fig. I.4).[3]

Here too the aim was to identify touch and apperception. The identification between vision and touch had not always been taken for granted. The apostle Thomas, for one, apparently dissociated seeing and touching. The proof of the seeing was, for him, in the touching. Yet the Gospel seems to have been unkindly disposed toward Thomas the toucher, the experimentalist, who was not content with trusting the simple evidence of his eyes.

In a way, the emblem of the eye in the palm of a hand relates to the biblical interdiction against dissociating touch and vision. "Ocula Fides" is the motto under Zincgref's seeing hand, and "Non temere credendum" is the motto around a similar hieroglyph in Alciati's *Emblemata.*[4] Touching is the modality of the believing eye; no actual contact with hand or fingertip is necessary.

Such emblems are far from being simple copies of Egyptian hieroglyphs. The mode of their construction by the graphic artist testifies to the presence of another operation: a process of transfer. In all the emblems with hand-inserted eyes the hand is no longer a limb, a *membrum,* that begins at the corner of the eye and is only a sort of ancillary appendix to the eye, as in the Egyptian hieroglyphs. It has become a supporting platform for the eye's action. In the Egyptian hieroglyph the hand existed before the eye and took its origin, its source, in the eye. In the pseudo hieroglyphs of emblematics, it is the eye that has left its original place, its socket, to nestle in the palm of the hand. This process of reversal reveals the sense of the transformation: now it is the hand that does things; the ancillary eye merely hangs from it as the remora from the shark's back. In the emblem the eye is merely a pilot guiding the hand toward

I.5 *Khamssa*, or hand against the evil eye.

its objectives; in the Egyptian hieroglyph, on the contrary, the eye-sun rules over the hand in an absolute manner, just as the pharaoh ruled over Egypt.

Another stage of development on the road toward the oculocentrism of Courbet and other French realists was folklore. In the Middle East and North Africa an amulet called a *khamssa*, or sometimes "Fatima's hand," has existed for centuries; indeed, one might consider it a translation into popular visual language of the long-forgotten *âri* hieroglyph. This hand too is endowed with an eye in the middle of the palm (fig. I.5).

The idea inherent in the *khamssa* doubtlessly is that of exorcising the evil eye. It embodies the sort of thinking which anthropologists call sympathetic magic. The very representation of the evil eye on the hand is believed to cause the look of any actual evil eye in one's vicinity to ricochet back on itself. The magic hand, the *khamssa*, mirrorlike, will hurl the evil spell back upon itself and blind the evil look.[5]

Another hieroglyph of sixteenth-century art that deserves mention here is the mannerist *Self-portrait* in a convex mirror of Parmigianino.[6] Mannerism was influenced by the development of emblems and indeed was perhaps the style in which emblematic activity reached its apex. In this portrait the curved mirror causes the hand of the painter in the foreground to become like a huge paw in relation to the body to which it belongs. Moreover, the mirror itself suggests a human eye. One might consider the whole picture as a new development of the emblem. The hand of the painter and the painter himself seem to be imprisoned in his own eye, so that the hand is no longer the container of the eye, as in earlier emblems, but is its containee. Is Parmigianino saying that *la bella maniera* necessarily implies the imprisonment of the artist inside the house of pure visuality?

Not until a century after Courbet's time was this concept of the prison house of visuality destroyed. The first great masterpiece of the surrealist cinema, *Un Chien Andalou* by Salvador Dali and Luis Buñuel, is primarily about vision and touch. One scene remains etched forever in the memory of anyone who has seen the film: the man holding a barber's razor in his hand and cutting off the eyeball of a beautiful young woman. In the very next sequence, a man's hand caresses the breast of a woman, probably the same woman to whom the mutilated eye belongs. Later, the man's hand is seen with a gaping hole in its palm, a sort of empty eye socket. Was it to enable the touching, the petting, of the breast that the eye had to be cut off? The eye perhaps was seen as a sort of weapon capable of preventing touch. Seeing is touching, to be sure; yet the eye of the woman one wishes to touch may prove to be an obstacle to the plenitude of touching.

A second masterpiece, written shortly before *Un Chien Andalou*, contains the key to this cinematographic philosophizing. Georges Bataille's short story "Histoire de l'oeil"—actually a philosophical essay on apperception as sexuality—is about a mutilated eye, an eye that sometimes takes the place of sex, being physically inserted into the locus of human sex, just as the emblematic eye is inserted into the palm of the human hand. As Bataille writes, "there are three things that the human eye is incapable of looking at: the sun, death and copulation." That was the discovery made also by Buñuel, who confessed to Bataille that he was sick for a whole day after shooting his terrible scene.[7]

Bataille was probably the first writer who, without actually using the term, defined the *scopic pulsion* that looms so large in the writings of Jacques Lacan.[8] For Lacan, too, seeing—any kind of seeing—is equated with sexual penetration of various degrees of intensity, and the regard directed upon the Other is explicitly described as an extension of the sexual thrust.

Optics and Haptics

The two fundamental categories, according to the art historian Alois Riegl, one of the great precursors of the semiotic approach to the visual arts, are optics and haptics.[9] Riegl stated that one type of artistic procedure, which corresponds to a certain way of looking, is based on the scanning of objects according to their outlines. This trajectory of the regard Riegl called the optical. The opposite type of vision, which focuses on surfaces and emphasizes the value of the superficies of objects, Riegl called the haptical (from the Greek *haptein*, "to seize, grasp," or *haptikos*, "capable of touching").

On the level of artistic creation, the optical look—if the eye belongs to a painter—produces linearity and angularity, whereas haptic creativity focuses on surfaces. Using Riegl's formula, all forms of art may be grouped under the heading "Outline and/or color in plane or volume" (*Umriss und/oder Farbe in Ebene oder Raum*). The optical eye merely brushes the surfaces of things. The haptic, or tactile, eye penetrates in depth, finding its pleasure in texture and grain.

Riegl was not the first philosopher and aesthetician to discern this dichotomy. Applying it to art analysis, turning the dichotomy into an art history concept, was his great achievement, but the concept of the haptic, the idea that vision is a form of touching, can be found earlier, in the work of Descartes and Berkeley.

In Descartes's treatise on dioptrics one reads: "The blind: one might say that they see through their hands. . . . Observe that the differences a blind person notices between trees, stones, water and other things of the kind through the agency of his stick are no less to him than the ones which differentiate red from yellow and green and which differentiate between all the other colors."[10] This passage may have been in the mind of Merleau-Ponty when he wrote that "the Cartesian model for vision is touch."[11]

More striking is Berkeley's model. For Berkeley, there is no vision in the performative meaning of the term—that is, in the sense of seeing as a potentiality of acting over the objects that surround us—without a transfer of the sense of touch to the operations of vision. The locating of the objects in the world and their identification—what today is called pattern recognition—and even more so the evaluation of the distance between the observing eye and the points of his focusing on the surface of these objects are synesthetic operations. The purely optical (without synesthesia) is only capable of apprehending points on a plane surface. "Visual appearances are altogether flat," Berkeley wrote.[12] It is only through a transference of the sense of touch to the eye that one is able to locate and identify things and evaluate one's position in relation to them. Purely optical vision by an eye devoid of the synesthetic sense of touch would be a vision without pattern recognition in which only points, or at best two-dimensional extension, would be perceived: "For distance being a line directed end-wise to the eye, it projects only one point in the fund of the eye, which point remains invariably the same, whether the distance be longer or shorter."[13] Even more than Descartes, then, Berkeley is the inventor of a conception of apperception based on a dual axis: the optical axis, through which what might be called nonepistemic vision is made possible, and the haptical axis, which in the act of actual seeing is projected onto the other one in an act of necessary synesthesia.[14]

The idea of the purely optical set against the purely haptical is also present under other names in Hegel's series of courses called *Aesthetics*.[15] Here one also encounters the dialectical idea—the idea that the history of artistic genres is the result of succeeding acts of negation and dialogue between the two poles of the dichotomy.

Our own period has seen the flourishing of so much research on the question of visual apperception that the Rieglian (later Wölfflinian) categories of optics and haptics have been made almost visible. In the Soviet Union, for instance, the physiologist A. L. Yarbus and in the United States the researchers David Noton and Lawrence Stark have done illuminating studies of eye movements in the perceiving of flat pictures.

The linear (optic) traces of an eye looking at a picture by Repin through seven bouts of scanning of twenty-five seconds each are shown in figure I.6, taken from Yarbus's work.[16] The picture being scanned, *The Unexpected (Nje Jdali)*, is reproduced in the upper left corner of the figure. It represents a political prisoner of the 1826 Decembrist movement returning from Siberia after a long exile and being greeted by his wife; his children, seated at the table, seem not to recognize him.

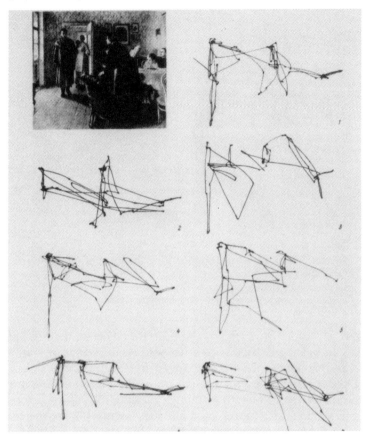

I.6 *The Unexpected* by Repin, followed by saccades representing scanning of the picture by seven pairs of eyes. From A. L. Yarbus, *Eye Movements in Vision.*
Copyright Plenum Press, New York; by permission.

The diagrams are formed by straight lines, called saccades, joining together two points of fixation. It is not exactly eye movements that have been recorded but rather those of the fovea within the retina—the spot of the retina that is endowed with the greatest concentration of photosensitive cells.[17] By placing the record of the saccades over a transparent paper and subsequently applying this paper over the surface of the reproduction of the painting, it is possible to see in detail how a person reads the picture.

The saccades represent the quick following of outlines; indeed, many of these saccades follow the lines of the floor, the door, the window. We are enabled to see the quick jumping over the outlines of things to establish relations between the persons and objects depicted in the painting. What we have here, then, is the fixed trace of an optical reading.

Another example from Yarbus's work shows how an eye optically reads the

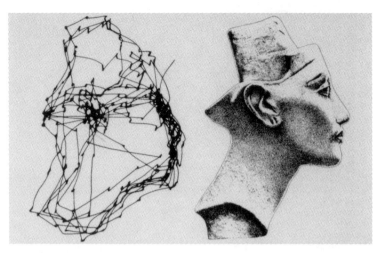

I.7 Scanning of a postcard representing the head of Nefertiti by eyes looking at it during three minutes. From A. L. Yarbus, *Eye Movements in Vision.*
Copyright Plenum Press, New York; by permission.

photograph of a sculpture, in this case a postcard depicting the head of Nefertiti (fig. I.7). In being projected onto a flat surface, the sculpture—an example of the tactile par excellence—was changed by the truly optical eye of the camera. Optical scanning by the human eye is shown proceeding in the flatness of the surface, not in depth as though piercing the surface orthogonally.

Yet haptic vision is also represented in these diagrams. It is concentrated in the points of fixation between the saccades. The importance of these zones comes to the fore more graphically in a study by Noton and Stark. The scanning of a picture by Paul Klee shows the importance of the fixation points in relation to the wavering saccades that link them (fig. I.8).

These points are rather like fairly large blots, and the extension of the black surfaces is due to the in-depth fixation of the observer's gaze as it was being printed on magnetic tape during the recording of the scanning path left by the fovea. These pools of darkness are the imprints of the touch of the eye when it ceased to jump with the linear saccades and remained fixed on specific spots, as if boring through the canvas or paper. They are the indices of the haptical element in the observer's gaze.

A Dual Axis

Riegl had several disciples, and not only in the art historical field. The German psychologist Viktor Lowenfeld attempted a classification of types of apperception in children according to Riegl's dichotomy. Lowenfeld posited

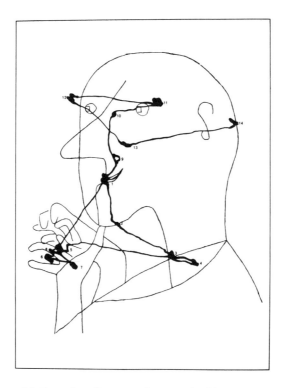

I.8 Scanning diagram of an eye looking at
Paul Klee's *Figuring Old Man.* From David
Noton and Lawrence Stark, "Eye Movements
and Visual Perception."
*By permission of Scientific American, Inc.,
and W. H. Freeman Co., New York.*

that there should be two fundamental types of creativity in children, the
optical and the haptical, the first proceeding through metaphor in its apprehension of things and jumping from one point to another point over the
surface of pictures and objects, the second proceeding according to contact
with the surface of things themselves. "The child who refers mainly to visual
experience, we call the 'visual' type whereas the other who refers mostly to
his own subjective feelings and to body and muscular feelings . . . we call
the 'haptic' type," Lowenfeld wrote.[18] Thus, just as there are two main axes
of visual touching, one of which really hardly touches the surface at all,
there are two antithetical types of children's vision.

Yet, doesn't thinking in terms of a linear–pictorial or optical–haptical dichotomy actually mean thinking in terms of another well-known dichotomy,
metaphor and metonymy? It was Roman Jakobson, following in the footsteps of Ferdinand de Saussure, who defined two main types of verbal asso-

ciations and verbal creation in children, the metaphoric and the metonymic. These types correspond to the two main axes of language defined in the linguistics of Saussure. Thus one child will proceed through jumps (from the Greek *metaphorein*, "to carry over") from one paradigm to another (so that, for example, a word like *shack* will be associated to *house* or *skyscraper*), while another child will associate through metonymic contact within a syntactic string (so that *shack* will be associated with a possible syntactic content, such as *has burned down, has been built, is made of wood*, etc.).

Could it not be claimed that optical scanning or reading of a picture (as in the reading of the Repin picture described by Yarbus) is of the metaphoric type? Does it not jump from spot to spot in order to establish relations between elements that are not necessarily in contact with each other? If one places the saccades of the Soviet observer on a transparent screen and transfers them onto the surface of *The Unexpected*, as I have done, one sees that the eye of the observer follows the floor lines and goes on to the left hand of the unexpected visitor, then jumps toward his right hand, then toward his eyes; from his eyes it goes to those of the two servants standing on the threshold, from them to the eyes of the woman and the children, and so on and on. The saccades establish a kind of bridge between semantic disparates: from floor to feet to hand to eye. This is a semantic reading of the picture. This painting is read by the eye of the observer as an icon in Peirce's sense, as a reproduction of reality based on resemblance and not as an index, as a sign that reveals a specific genre or technique or the style of a particular painter or school.

A haptical reading would, on the contrary, fixate the fovea on the surfaces and grounds and backgrounds, on the texture, the coloring. Such a reading trajectory would resemble the drippings of Jackson Pollock rather than the seismographic saccades seen in the Yarbus diagrams. And indeed, doesn't the surface of the Klee drawing in figure I.8 present a type of eye trajectory that resembles the drippings of action painting? It must be said that the linearity of quick saccades is also present in the work of Pollock and that his work combines both haptic drippings and seismographic optics. However that may be, this type of haptic touching reads a picture nonsemantically, as an index of the painter's hand, of his technique and style, as signature rather than representation.

All types of regard, whether of a reader or of a painter, proceed along these two antithetical lines. Such double scanning, at once touching and jumping, is perhaps a translation into the pictorial modality of the language dichotomy described by Jakobson.

Ancient Egypt, where the eye-god was a pure performative and literally caused things and events to exist, produced a painting style that was almost purely optical. As a matter of fact, the Egyptian painter did not *see*—or rather, saw only into his inner self or into the sacred codes he had internalized. He never claimed to be observing reality. The hieroglyph representing the all-touching eye of Courbet, on the contrary, coexisted with the doctrine of realism, with the theory that things exist in themselves as autonomous entities and create apperception rather than being created by it. Courbet, a painter who aimed primarily at touching things with his eye, was, paradoxically, the creator of texture and surface effects, not the mere receptor of an existing reality.

As Hegel suggested, the chronological succession of pictorial movements may be described in dialectical terms: the purity of classical antiquity was succeeded by Roman kitsch (*Kunstindustrie*, in Riegl's terminology), medieval dogmatism by Renaissance liberalism, Renaissance harmonics by the distorted shapes of mannerism and the baroque. It is this dialectic that develops through the ages from the interaction of the optic and the haptic. The process is suggested in Riegl's description of the art works of antiquity: of optic Egypt and haptic Greece, of optic Greece and the more haptic Rome.[19]

If one considers the modern period, the same dialectical process applies. The quarrel in the French Academy during the baroque between followers of Rubens (advocates of surface and color) and followers of Poussin (advocates of outline and drawing) was an expression of that process. So was the subsequent quarrel between the neoclassicist exponents of the pure line and the romanticists who upheld the doctrine of texture and tachism. The continuing struggle saw the aesthetic triumph of haptics in the doctrines of the impressionist movement, but optics reappeared in the linearity of pictorial symbolism. In our own day we have seen the predominantly haptic qualities of abstract expressionism evolve by degrees into the art of the pure line and flat colors—that is, into pop art.

Touching the Text

And what about literature? The eye does not read only pictures; it also reads texts. The eye does not touch only the texture of painting; it also scans the surfaces of written texts.

Once again the work of Yarbus provides an example, one of the few experiments made of the scanning of a poem by a human eye (fig. I.9). But the diagram shows a very linear and obedient reading, word after word, line after line. Yarbus tells us that the reader was not reading out of pleasure but was a hired student, willing to read any text handed to him as a necessary part of the experiment.

As for me, I am conscious of reading texts in quite a different manner, usually at great speed. My reading is jumpy, full of forward flashes and backward glances. Such a scanning—the type of scanning intellectual workers usually carry out—has been recorded by another researcher, the American E. Llewellyn Thomas (fig. I.10).[20] This diagram is an instance of speed

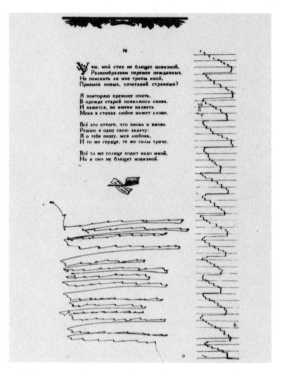

I.9 Scanning by a student of a Shakespeare
sonnet (in Russian). From A. L. Yarbus,
Eye Movements in Vision.
Copyright Plenum Press, New York; by permission.

reading. But even in the literary researcher's patient deciphering of a text, I
doubt that one could obtain the type of eye movement recorded by Yarbus.
The true decipherer is the person who runs through a text in a jumping,
"metaphoric" manner, establishing connections between words that are far
apart and not necessarily following the order ostensibly imposed upon the
eye by the sequential succession of lines.

I reiterate: one should speak of two fundamental axes of visual scanning,
whether it is texts or pictures that are being read. One axis is that of metaphoric, optic scanning, which proceeds through semantic jumps from one
corner of the picture or text to another. The other axis is that of haptic or
contact vision, which bores through texture and color and fixes on nonse-
mantic elements in picture or text. Such a deconstruction of picture or text
into a twofold structure gives the fullest legitimacy to the linguistic or semiotic approach used by contemporary researchers in their analyses. This kind
of approach will be used in the next chapter, in which the notion of speech
act will be transferred from the province of pure linguistic analysis to
painting.

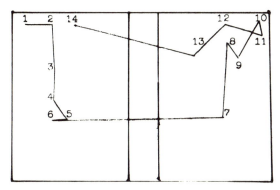

I.10 An eye reading a text at great speed.
Diagram by the author, after E. Llewellyn Thomas,
"Eye Movements in Speed Reading," in R. G.
Stauffer, ed., Speed Reading: Practices and
Procedures, *University of Delaware Press, 1962.*

II

THE GESTURE OF DEMONSTRATION

In one particular corpus of paintings belonging to the quattrocento, the pre-Renaissance period in Italy (ca. 1450–1500), a specific gesture is omnipresent: a hand with its index finger pointing toward an object within the painting (fig. II.1). This gesture did not exist in the iconography of the Western world before the fifteenth century, and it became rare after 1490.

I call this motion of the hand and index finger the gesture of demonstration. I borrowed the term from Bertolt Brecht. By practicing the *Gestus des Zeigens* Brechtian actors are supposed to foreground the showing element in their acting instead of the illusionist element. Thus they show that they are showing, or demonstrating, existential possibilities, not embodying real persons.

In painting, the gesture of demonstration is rhetorical, directed toward the spectator. It is an appeal signal, inviting the spectator to look in a specific direction or at a specific object inside the representation.

The word *appeal* evokes another semiotic complex related to showing, the trilogy of language functions first defined by Karl Bühler: expression/representation/appeal.[1] Wolfgang Iser later brought to the fore the essential role played by the third, the appeal element, in textual works of art.[2] The present chapter aims to point up the appeal element chiefly in visual works of art but also in written texts.

The gesture of demonstration made by a character depicted in a quattrocento painting not only appeals to us to focus our attention on a particular object or detail inside the painting. It also, by virtue of its merely being there as an important element in the painting, proclaims the whole picture to be an appeal structure and not an illusion of reality. Of course, this Brechtian

II.1 Pointing hand.
Drawing by the author.

14

II.2 *Sacra Conversazione* by Piero della Francesca.
By permission of the Brera Museum.

gesture of demonstration does not embrace the totality of functions present in quattrocento pictures. But the appeal function is certainly dominant among them.

The Corpus

The pictures I have chosen to illustrate this phenomenon are a *Sacra Conversazione* by Piero della Francesca at the Brera Museum (fig. II.2), a *Sacra Conversazione* by Domenico Veneziano at the Ufizzi in Florence (fig. II.3), the *Virgin and Child with Saints Dominic, John the Baptist, Peter Martyr, and*

II.3 *Sacra Conversazione* by Domenico Veneziano.
Diagram by the author.

Thomas Aquinas by Fra Angelico at the San Marco Museum in Florence (fig. II.4), the *Virgin and Child with Saints Peter Martyr, Damiano, John the Evangelist, Laurence, and Francis* by the same artist and in the same museum (fig. II.5), and the *Trinity* by Masaccio in the Santa Maria Novella church in Florence (fig. II.6).

In three of these pictures the part of the demonstrator, or designator, is given to Saint John the Baptist. In one instance it is played by Saint John the Evangelist and in one instance by the Virgin Mary. In a number of quattrocento pictures outside this corpus that I have had an opportunity to examine, a high proportion of designators are Saint John the Baptist figures. Later in this chapter I will discuss the significance of this phenomenon—of the Baptist as demonstrator par excellence—to Christian theology.

From Expositor to Demonstrator

Especially interesting are figures II.4 and II.5, which show that the designator is located in a spatial plane totally different from that which contains the designatum, the designated figure or object. Even the scale of representation of the designator differs from that of the designated object (in both cases the designatum is the Virgin and Child). That suggests to me that this figure may have been transposed to painting from the late medieval stage. The figure may

II.4 *Virgin and Child with Saints Dominic, John the
Baptist, Peter Martyr, and Thomas Aquinas* (detail)
by Fra Angelico.
By permission of the San Marco Museum, Florence.

have come from a tableau vivant; similar transpositions have been documented by research on the period.[3] Indeed, the late medieval stage, especially the genre of tableaux vivants, used an actor who was Brechtian in the sense already defined—a demonstrator. This actor was called the expositor (fig. II.7).

The function of the expositor was to stand on the proscenium with a rule in his hand, designate for the benefit of the audience each of the silent actors who stood frozen on the stage, and comment on the allegorical content of each figure represented. As figure II.7 shows, this proscenium was unlike the one on which the Virgin and Child are seen in figures II.4 and II.5. Thus the borrowing of a real stage character and his function of demonstration—if such a borrowing did indeed occur—must have been accompanied by an inversion of the function played by the proscenium, for in figures II.4 and II.5 it is the object designated that is on a sort of proscenium, while the designator stands among his peers.

II.5 *Virgin and Child with Saints Peter Martyr,*
Damiano, John the Evangelist, Laurence, and Francis
(detail) by Fra Angelico.
By permission of the San Marco Museum, Florence.

The Speech Act Model

The expositor or demonstrator causes us to look at the sacred object on the stage or in the picture. This ordering us about by the demonstrator suggests that a semiotic model may also be applicable here. I have in mind the Austinian, or speech act, model.[4]

According to J. L. Austin, some ordinary speech enunciations are mere

II.6 *Trinity* (detail) by Masaccio.
Author's photograph.

reports or comments on the state of things or on actions performed—a kind of taking stock. Such locutionary enunciations are called constatives. Other enunciations actually do something or cause someone to do something. They are called performatives. The minister who pronounces two persons man and wife performs an act through the mere uttering of a sentence. Similarly, the queen who christens a ship "I name you the *Formidable*" actually performs an act. All sentences of this type—which actually do something— form a subclass within the general category of the performatives. Austin calls the subclass illocutionary. The other subclass of utterances, the ones that cause someone to do something, is called perlocutionary.

A painting which proclaims that it is showing something (and not creating the illusionistic appearance of the thing) thus is performing an illocutionary speech act, while a painting which tells us to look at a specific point within itself is performing a perlocutionary act. Both types of acts are being performed in the pictures belonging to our corpus.

Constative, or locutionary, gestures and motions within pictures are those directed by a represented figure toward another represented figure within the picture plane. Such gestures are not directed toward an outside observer

II.7 Tableau vivant with an expositor on
the proscenium.
Diagram by the author.

or spectator and are not for his benefit. Since the beginning of the High
Renaissance (the period that followed the quattrocento) the majority of pictures have been of this type. As Michel Foucault wrote in his analysis of the
Meninas of Velasquez, this type of representation behaves as though it were
not the object of external observation; it is a simulacrum of reality, as though
"pure visibility [could] represent itself."[5]

Pictures of the constative type interpose a sort of transparent fourth wall,
a screen, between the audience and the picture plane. This transposition
produces the *Guckkasteneffekt*, the illusionistic peeping-box effect described
by Brecht apropos of the Italian stage. The effect is said to be negative, not to
be desired, because the characters on stage, the actors, perform in bad faith,
pretending they are not seen while knowing all along that they are being
watched by spectators. The spectator too is placed in a situation of bad
faith—the situation of a person who watches through a keyhole. It is precisely this bad faith that Brecht sought to abolish through his technique of
direct appeal to the external observer.

The pictorial gesture of demonstration, belonging as it does to this Brechtian technique, falls into the province of the illocutionary. Through gesticulation, the demonstrator not only speaks directly to us about an object he is showing us but also makes a statement about his action (which he reveals as an act of designation). In addition, he speaks to us about the painting that contains him as a represented figure; he reveals it as a showing rather than a mimesis, or representation.

Illocutionary and Perlocutionary Functions

The performative functions of the gesture of demonstration in our corpus of quattrocento paintings may be divided into two illocutionary functions, *distancing (I1)* and *indexing (I2)*, and two perlocutionary functions, *gaze directing (P1)* and *ideological directing (P2)*. For reasons that I shall subsequently discuss, the second perlocutionary function may be further subdivided, into an *empathizing* function *(P2a)*.

Distancing (I1)

The first illocutionary function is the Brechtian one. The demonstrator, or designator, in the picture is telling the spectator, "I am showing you an enunciation," "I am showing you that I am showing you." Through the *Gestus des Zeigens* it is the painting as a whole which declares, "I am showing." The painting in its totality proclaims itself to be a *presentation* and not a *representation*. By virtue of their containing a designator, the paintings in our corpus declare that they are presenting a religious reality and are not representations of it.

And that, Giovanni-Battista Alberti tells us in his treatise *On Painting*, is how art should be:

> I like to see in a painting a figure which admonishes us and designates with its finger that which is taking place inside the picture; or one which makes us a sign with its hand for us to watch something that is occurring [inside]; or which, with a choleric complexion and sparkling eyes, threatens us that we should not come near; or which points to some danger or miracle represented in the picture. Thus, all that is happening between the characters is shown and designated as ornament or lesson.[6]

Indexing (I2)

Through the distancing function, our quattrocento paintings assert their relationship to the distanced medieval stage, as we have already seen. At the same time, the pictures put forward an indexing character in relation to the divine. They are indices of the divine, not representations of it. They assert the presence of Christ.

As a matter of fact, the act of demonstration is the most basic of Christian acts. The word *martus* in koine Greek means "witness." The Christian martyr is primarily a demonstrator whose function is to point toward Christ and his divinity. The martyr points toward Christ with his index finger and with his own martyrdom, which is also an index of the divine. That is why Saint John the Baptist is the archetypal demonstrator: he is the archmartyr, the first person put to death as a witness of Christ.

Through this *Gestus* of the finger extended toward the person of Christ, the designator also proclaims the nonessential character of his own person and the all-essential character of his designatum. The Christian demonstrators (those who are represented in our corpus) always proclaim, "I am nothing, look at the essential object my fingertip is designating!"

This image of the pointing finger was used in the writings of the church fathers. For example, Saint Augustine writes in *De doctrina Christiana:*

> I say that it is not I who am at fault if certain persons do not understand what I write. For if I should point out to them with my finger the old or the new moon and they should not be able to see it, they should not reproach me with their failure. Similarly, those who have studied the precepts and remain without understanding . . . think they can see my finger but not the Holy Scriptures which this finger intended to designate. Those two groups should cease to accuse me, since I can only raise my finger toward something in order to point it out to them but am not capable of giving them the vision which makes one see both the gesture and object it is designating.

Augustine criticized those who took the gesture of demonstration for the thing itself, for the designatum, and could not perceive this designatum because it was located beyond all possibilities of representation and could only be captured through vision.

Augustine's words are based on similar words in the Gospel of John (3:30), the words of the first demonstrator and expositor, John the Baptist, who summed up his witnessing of Christ with the phrase "illum opportet crescere me autem minui" ("in order for him to grow, I must diminish"). These words are, of course, ambiguous. They refer to John's approaching beheading, his literal diminishing, but they are also a proper description of the designator-martyr as a nonessential index of the essential: in order that others be able to see Christ, I, the demonstrator, must disappear as a person, must remain as a *Gestus des Zeigens*, a mere index.

Interestingly, there is a major work of Renaissance art that illustrates this indexing function. The famous Colmar triptych by Grünewald— which belongs chronologically to the Renaissance (1513) but is rooted spiritually in late medieval Christianity—shows, on its central panel beneath the crucifixion of Christ, the sentence "illum opportet crescere me autem minui" in large letters. Beside it is the pointing index finger of John the Baptist (fig. II.8). It is as though the painting in its totality were

II.8 *Crucifixion* by Matthias Grünewald
(detail). Isenheimer Altar.
Photo Musée Unterdenlinden, Colmar.

proclaiming, "I must diminish *qua representatio* in order to grow *qua designatio.*"

The indexing function of a painting actually is tantamount to smashing it as an icon. There is indeed in the Grünewald painting, as in our quattrocento corpus, an aspiration to be an index, which I would not hesitate to contrast with the iconic aspirations of High Renaissance painting. After 1500, as a rule, the objective was pure representation, the creation of pure icons or mirrors of nature. In Foucault's words, "pure visibility represents itself." The ultimate aim was to create images so perfect that all traces of the enunciative process would be absent from the *énoncé*, the picture itself.

There is such a telescopic embedding of indices in the Grünewald painting that further comment is warranted. In addition to John the Baptist pointing toward the inscription below the cross and to Christ on the cross (fig. II.9), a Saint Sebastian figure in the right-hand panel makes a sublimated motion of designation in the direction of the central panel. I say sublimated, for this

II.9 Central panel of Grünewald's
Crucifixion.
Photo Musée Unterdenlinden, Colmar.

character is painted as though his left hand were keeping his right hand from carrying out the *Gestus*. If Sebastian is Grünewald's own portrait, as generally assumed, then the painter himself functions as an index. Furthermore, the body on the cross—quite clearly a cadaver, a swollen container—is also an index of the divine presence. Thus a painter-martyr points to a saint-martyr (the Baptist) who points to an inscription and an index (the ultimate index, the cadaver). In fact, in the Grünewald painting the function of the pointing index finger must be extended to the totality. The triptych as a whole proclaims, "I am an index pointing to Christ."

But it is not just our quattrocento corpus and the Grünewald painting; for any painting done in a Christian spirit, being an index is a sign of authenticity and value. Any painting that proclaims itself to be more index than icon participates to some extent in the glory of the Veronica, the *vera icona*, the

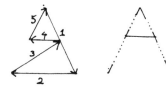

II.10 Scan-path of an observer's eye
looking at an A-shape.
Diagram by the author.

true icon—true precisely because it is no icon at all but an imprint of the face of Christ. This aspiration to the condition of index or trace (the Veronica is the trace left by the face of Christ in the shroud), contains in itself an ideological trace, the trace of its theological origin. It expresses the force of the Mosaic proscription against making graven images and reveals the Judaic matrix at the heart of Christian representation.

Indeed, Christianity is a series of indexing gestures, starting with the *ecce agnus dei* uttered by John the Baptist, continuing with the *ecce homo* uttered by Pontius Pilate, and corrected by the *ecce deus* expressed by the pointing index fingers of the apostles. A semiotic description of the series—that is, of the telescopic organization of such indices—would be tantamount to a description of Christian dogma.

Gaze Directing (P1)

I now turn to the second group of functions, the perlocutionary ones. These functions aim not at expressing the intention of doing or performing something through saying or representing it but at provoking the external observer into doing something as a consequence of observing the picture.

The gesture of the hand with the pointing finger is a vector (as Umberto Eco defined it in his general treatise on semiotics[7]). It captures the gaze of the observers and literally directs it toward a point in the picture plane. This gaze-directing function has long been noted by students of human perception, especially by Yarbus and by Noton and Stark.[8]

The latter researchers demonstrated that in each visual configuration, be it simple or complex, there exists a built-in trajectory for the observer's gaze. This trajectory, called the scan-path, is invariable, at least in the case of simple configurations. Scanning an A-shape of large dimensions thus can be invariably described as a 1—2—3—4—5 trajectory carried out by the eye (figure II.10).

In the same way, the paintings which contain a demonstrator may be said to present a built-in scan-path (fig. II.11). The gaze of the demonstrator creates the first segment, establishing contact between his eyes or finger and the eyes of the external observer. The pointing finger of this demonstrator then creates a second vector between its tip and the designatum. Thus, in the

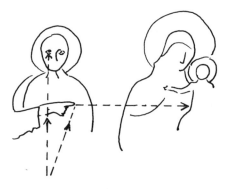

II.11 Scan-path of an observer's eye
looking at a quattrocento demonstrator.
Diagram by the author.

paintings of the quattrocento containing a demonstrator, scan-paths of the type shown in figure II.11 can always be found. I call the establishing of such a trajectory the gaze-directing function.

Ideological Directing (P2)

The second perlocutionary function corresponds to the illocutionary function of indexing. Rather than proclaiming the picture's own indexing character, however, the aim of this function is to make the viewer a Christian witness, a martyr. It aims to cause militancy in favor of the Christian cause.

It is perhaps in this sense that Alberti's statement about his liking for paintings that admonish us should be interpreted. "I like to see a figure which admonishes us and designates with its finger that which is happening within a picture" might be read not only as a discourse on techniques of representation but also as a statement in favor of Christian militancy—as though Alberti were saying, "We observers should be like this figure which points toward the representation of Christ; we too should be demonstrators and pointers."

Empathizing (P2a)

And yet Alberti's treatise eventually moves toward empathy, toward the empathic perlocutionary function. After giving vent to his taste for the figure of the demonstrator located inside a painting, Alberti adds that he likes these figures "because they invite us to weep with them or laugh with them." Here we no longer have a plea in favor of militancy but an exaltation of the self-identification of the viewer with the figure of the demonstrator. We should, Alberti is saying, behave emotionally, like the designator.

This part of the Alberti text is a straightforward piece of Aristotelianism, even though it comes after a really non-Aristotelian stance; art appreciation is now said to be a mimesis of the emotional content portrayed in the art work. The Alberti text has moved from Brechtlike didacticism to the antithetical pole of mimesis and empathy. I would surmise that Alberti's treatise marks a turning point, a watershed: the dividing line where quattracento art is about to fall into the doctrine of realism, mimetic illusion.

A Hierarchy of Functions

I have defined the quattrocento pictures as conglomerates of functions. But in what way does such a conglomerate achieve its functioning as a totality? Is there a hierarchy in the order in which the four or five functions I have defined operate?

My presentation of the various speech act functions of painting began with the illocutionary and finished with the perlocutionary, the same order in which Austin presented his model in *How to Do Things with Words*. It is probable, however, that the perlocutionary force of a painting is the first force felt by an observer. Thus the gaze-directing function (P1) would come first. Then would come ideological directing (P2). The Albertinian, or Aristotelian, mimetic-emotional function (P2a) might then take over. It would be only later, on a second, in-depth reading, that the illocutionary, metapictorial functions of distancing (I1) and indexing (I2) would be perceived, as the picture speaks about itself and about its own functioning as a sign of demonstration. The hierarchy of the functions operating in the course of a total reading of a picture, then, would follow the pattern P1—P2—P2a—I1—I2.

Another possibility is that the set of functions operates in a metastable manner, in a pattern that links the perlocutionary and the illocutionary according to a reversible polar structure.[9] In this case, gaze-directing–distancing (P1–I1) and ideological directing/empathizing–indexing (P2/P2a–I2) would form two reversible couples in which the perlocutionary and the illocutionary aspects would succeed one another in a perpetual oscillation. This pendulumlike functioning would constitute a sort of *va-et-vient*, flip-flop structure.

Proxemics

The gesture of demonstration is not a mere ancillary motion accompanying a series of semantic injunctions. It exists in space and is spatially extended on the surface of a canvas. It therefore belongs to the semiotic of spatial organization, to proxemics.

Let me recall the definition of the gesture with the pointing hand as it was

formulated by Eco.[10] For him the gesture of demonstration belongs to the
category *ostention,* the category of indicial signs of a noniconic character
endowed with both syntactic and semantic marks.[11] The syntactic marks are
longitude, apicality, movement, dynamic force; the semantic marks are direction, proximity, distance. According to Eco, the ostention vectors contained by a painting or a surface confer a measure of toposensibility to this
surface.

Using Eco's terminology, we can say that the demonstrator confers on the
pictures a toposensibility that conflicts with the general perspectivist toposensibility. In the quattrocento corpus the motion of the hand with the
pointing finger directs our gaze along a lateral-horizontal axis, a direction
absolutely opposed to the direction of perspective space, in which the lines
converge orthogonally toward a vanishing point located in-depth. We can
also say that the quattrocento stage represented in these paintings was a
period of conflict in which the illusionism of the High Renaissance and its
aesthetic of the fourth wall and the *Guckkasten* had not yet triumphed. Such
a conflict makes manifest the interdependence of the ideological and the
semiotic. It was the presence of the indexing aspiration in quattrocento
painting, the aspiration to create works existing primarily as indices and not
as icons, that temporarily prevented the complete triumph of perspective.

The hegemony of the new Italianate perspective eventually turned the
representation of Christian dogma into a set of illusion-creating procedures,
which reached their most influential stage during the baroque period and
the Counter-Reformation. Demonstration disappeared as such. Figures in
paintings now made motions of demonstration that were no longer of the
illocutionary or perlocutionary type but were purely locutionary, intended
for characters inside the painting, not for the viewer (fig. II.12).

Moreover, the High Renaissance brought a triumph of the purely iconic, in
which all traces of the enunciative process were erased within the *énoncé.*
The finished product could no longer bear in an overt and visible manner
the traces of its own production. Such traces had to be eradicated. In addition, the gestures or motions in the act of pseudo communication followed
the general perspective direction, being oriented more or less in the general
direction of the vanishing point. Thus they were ancillary to the overall
perspective.

Metamorphoses

The transformations undergone by the gesture of demonstration from the
quattrocento to the present day may now be traced.

Although the gesture of demonstration—in the sense of an illocutionary
self-designation—became a rarity in Italian painting after 1490, there are
exceptions. The famous *Saint John the Baptist* by Leonardo, in which the

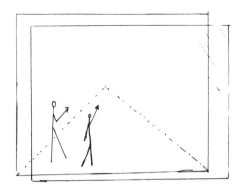

II.12 *Guckkasteneffekt* and pseudo
gestures of demonstration.
Diagram by the author.

Baptist points heavenward while gazing directly toward the spectator, is a
case in point. Another is Raphael's *Madonna da Foligno,* in which the Baptist
again is a demonstrator, soliciting the gaze of the observer while pointing
upward toward the ascending Virgin and Child, much as Leonardo's Baptist
does.

In these two instances, one may note that the gesture with the pointing
index finger has undergone a sort of syntactic change. Whereas the *Gestus
des Zeigens* in its truly Brechtian quattrocento form is a horizontal vector
extended in a direction parallel to the lower edge of the painting, that is,
without any vertical apicality (while the semantic marking "proximity" is
emphasized through the closeness between designator and designatum), in
the High Renaissance this gesture is almost completely vertical and apical;
yet the semantic marker "distance" reaches its maximum intensity: in the
Leonardo painting, *nothing*—no visible "thing"—is shown.

In the baroque period there is a famous painting with a demonstrator who
is almost a copy of the quattrocento demonstrators: the young page in El
Greco's *Burial of the Count of Orgaz.* He is looking at the outside observer
much in the same way the pre-Renaissance demonstrators look. Moreover, a
piece of paper emerges from the youth's pocket. On it the signature of the
painter is written, followed by the inscription "I made this."[12] It is not clear
whether El Greco refers to his authorship of the painting, but art historians
have observed that the date which follows the signature, 1578, is not that of
the finishing of the painting or the signing of the contract between the
sponsors of the work and the painter. It has been suggested that it must
therefore be the birth date of the page with the extended hand, and that the
artist was thereby referring to his paternity of the boy. Here the gesture of
demonstration accompanies the ostention of the signature, as though El
Greco intended to tell us that in matters of paternity, artistic or otherwise,

II.13 *Quo Vadis?* by Annibale Carraci.
Diagram by the author.

auctoritas, like the divinity of Christ, is ultimately that which is designated by a witness.

Spatial projection of the plane of representation itself toward the spectator can be found in Italian painting of the period. A case in point is the *Supper at Emmaus* by Caravaggio, in which a fruit basket in the foreground is balanced on the extreme edge of the table behind which Christ is sitting. This basket, it has been observed, is actually at the point of falling from the table, a fact revealed by the shadows this basket casts on the tablecloth. One could say in a somewhat daring metaphor that what we have here is a sort of visual eucharist: Christ projecting his own space toward us so that we might enter it.

Numerous paintings and sculptural groups of the baroque period produce such an effect. For example, Carraci's *Quo Vadis?* has the hand of the pointing Christ jutting out toward the viewer, signifying the only direction capable of leading a sinner toward redemption (fig. II.13).

Baroque realism manifests the same tendency of the picture to invade the spectator's space. The jutting out of objects, faces, and hands can be found in seventeenth-century Dutch painting. A well-known example is *The Smokers* by Brouwer, in which smoke appears to be blown in the viewer's face.

II.14 *Saint John the Baptist* by Philippe de Champaigne.
Photo Musée des Beaux Arts, Grenoble; by permission.

The effect sought after here doubtlessly is not a sort of visual eucharist but rather the provocation of the spectator. The smoke blower functions as a clown. Instead of being engulfed in sacred space the viewer is engulfed in a haze of reality.

Even in the baroque period certain trends ran counter to the pure illusionistic effects sought by Counter-Reformation artists. One such current was Jansenism, with its exalting of the hidden character of God. One might even say that Jansenism strove to create a de-iconized imagery that opposed the illusionistic-iconic baroque. This trend may be seen in particular in a painting by Philippe de Champaigne, *Saint John the Baptist* (fig. II.14).[13]

In this picture the gesture of demonstration is performed in a direction opposite to the one in the eucharistic space projection in baroque painting. The pointing hand of the Baptist rotates by an angle of 180 degrees in relation to the gesture in the *Emmaus* and the *Quo Vadis?* The person of the

II.15 *I Want You for U.S. Army* by
James Montgomery Flagg.
Author's photograph.

demonstrator again emerges as a prominent feature. This gesture of demonstration has an orthogonal-internal orientation, not the orthogonal-external orientation in the *Emmaus* and the *Quo Vadis?*

Furthermore, a designated Christ in figure II.14 is almost invisible; the viewer sees a mere silhouette, a mere trace of the divine, so that Christ himself becomes a sign of the ineffability of God. The figure of the demonstrator has reemerged precisely because Jansenist ideology emphasized the hidden character of God, *deus absconditus*. For the Jansenists, the only sign of the divine that can legitimately be depicted is the gesture of demonstration.

Leaving the baroque period, I jump precariously over three centuries to arrive at a picture which some might call the archetypal sign of the first part of this century—the famous picture sketched by J. M. Flagg in 1917 (fig. II.15). Here Uncle Sam is pointing orthogonally toward the space in front of the picture, the space in which the spectator is standing. His gesture is made explicit by the inscription.

At first, this poster seems to belong in the same class with the paintings we have read from the baroque period. The essential difference is that the baroque pictures are illusionist, realistic. Even if the fourth wall is shattered by the jutting hands of the disciples of Christ and by the falling fruit basket,

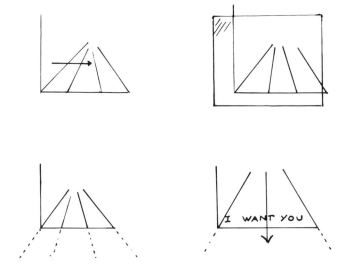

II.16 Four rotations of the pointing hand.
Diagram by the author.

the depicted characters never look us in the eye; the appeal function is not overt but hidden. The World War I poster, on the contrary, does not claim to be a serious representation. In fact, it de-iconizes itself through the sketchy character of its lines and the foregrounding of its appeal structure.

At the same time, it is truly a representation of the ambiguity of the I/you enunciation as described by Benvéniste.[14] Indeed, the I of the inscription "I WANT YOU FOR U.S. ARMY" is also the YOU with which it has changed places, since the American people Uncle Sam is supposed to stand for are also the spectator, the I who is reading this poster, here and now.

This foregrounded coexistence of an illocutionary stance juxtaposed to a perlocutionary action—having someone do something—seems to me to be a characteristic of modern publicity and modern art, both of which are primarily Brechtian in character. Both present themselves as a sort of theater of the enunciative process. Again a late medieval, or pre-Renaissance, technique is being "revived." The poster projects a slogan, just as Brecht's stage projects written inscriptions on banners or backdrops, corresponding to the *tituli* of medieval illuminations and paintings.

A series of diagrams may help to sum up the metamophoses of the gesture of demonstration. Figure II.16 shows the four main rotations of the pointing hand which form the full circle of all the demonstrating possibilities.

During the pre-Renaissance (top left) the demonstration takes place along horizontal lines, which run counter to the orthogonal perception of perspectival space. Simultaneously a vector of appeal links the gaze of the demonstrator to that of the external observer.

Et mefmement la cite tant ioffie,
Treffameufe dicte aquilepa
Par les hongres z feur roy athilla

II.17 Fragment of *L'Entreprise de Venise* by Pierre
Gringoire, showing a designating hand.
By permission of the Bibliothèque Nationale, Paris.

In the High Renaissance (top right) the demonstration is no longer a true demonstration. It is an imitation, or mimesis, of gestural language, taking place behind the fourth wall. The gesticulation does not run counter to perspectival space but is generally oriented in-depth as it follows the perspective lines converging toward the vanishing point.

In the baroque (lower left), as in the High Renaissance, the gesticulation is no longer a demonstration. No vector links the eyes of a demonstrator to the eyes of an external observer. But the gesticulation points in the orthogonal direction, not in-depth; it goes from the inside toward the space of the external observer. It has become ancillary to the projection of the space of representation onto the space of observation.

In the modern poster (lower right)—and, I would suggest, in modern art generally—the gesticulation is in the inward–outward direction, as during the baroque. Yet the illocutionary function and the appeal function are foregrounded. The picture is de-iconized through the presence of an inscription (a verbal enclave inside the visual) and through the "non finito" character of the drawing.

The Gesture in Literature

Many medieval and Renaissance manuscripts contain sketches of pointing hands. Hands and fingers drawn by scribes point to particular words or particular passages in a text, as in an example from the manuscript of Pierre Gringoire, *L'Entreprise de Venise* (fig. II.17).[15]

The study of these pointing fingers and their function is fascinating in itself, but I intend to deal here only with the idea of the pointing finger, the metaphor of the designating hand. I consider this pointing hand to be equivalent to the direct address to readers used by many authors. The overt telling of a story by a self-designating author corresponds to pointing with the finger, whereas the showing of scenes and actions by a realist writer does not.

Overt telling is frequent in much Renaissance literature, such as the prologues of Rabelais. It echoes the gesture of demonstration in the quattrocento paintings we have examined, and both can be said to derive from the didactic attitude that prevailed in the fifteenth century, with its tableaux vivants, its preoccupation with the scientific exploration of the universe, and its cartographic discoveries.

Another period in which this pointing finger was foregrounded in literature was the eighteenth century. Diderot's *Jacques le fataliste* and *Le Neveu de Rameau* are full of direct address to the reader, and so is Sterne's *Tristram Shandy*:

> But courage! gentle reader!—I scorn it—'tis enough to have thee in my power—but to make use of the advantage which the fortune of the pen has now gained over thee, would be too much—No—! by that all-powerful fire which warms the visionary brain, and lights the spirits through unworldly tracts! ere I would force a helpless creature upon this hard service, and make thee pay, poor soul! for fifty pages, which I have no right to sell thee—naked as I am, I would browse upon the mountains, and smile that the north wind brought me neither my tent or my supper . . . [16]

Even more forceful are Sterne's injunctions to an imaginary woman reader: "How could you Madam, be so inattentive in reading the last chapter? . . . I do insist upon it that you immediately turn back that is, as soon as you get to the next full stop, and read the whole chapter over again."[17]

Fielding's *Tom Jones* also includes dialogues with the reader:

> We are now, reader, arrived at the last stage of our long journey. As we have, therefore, travelled together through so many pages, let us behave to one another like fellow-travellers in a stagecoach, who have passed several days in the company of each other. . . . And now my friend, I take this opportunity (as I shall have no other) of heartily wishing thee well. If I have been an entertaining companion to thee, I promise thee it is what I have desired. If in anything I have offended, it was really without my intention.[18]

This is not only great comedy. These passages are also implicitly theoretical discourses. They foreground the appeal element in the text, revealing the literary text for what it is, or should be: an enunciation and not an *énoncé*; that is, a work in progress, a creative process in action rather than a finished product. They destroy any illusion of reality.

Brechtian aesthetics also were prefigured in Diderot's *Paradoxe sur le comédien*, an essay that advocated distance (although not, perhaps, the showing of distance—that was Brecht's invention) between an actor and his part as the best device to attain excellence in acting.[19]

The overt presence of the writers paradoxically became tantamount to obliteration of their presence as persons. Readers now saw working authors; they saw "how it was done," the creative process, the craft of literature; they no longer saw living persons behind the texts. The author's pointing finger, like Renaissance perspective, led the reader irresistibly toward a vanishing point, and this vanishing point was the person of the author.

III

PENETRATING DOORS

Doors in pictures, like pointing fingers, are performatives, gaze-directing devices. The preceding chapter focused on the manner in which an observer's gaze reaches the canvas as a response to an appeal directed toward the observer by a represented demonstrator. We saw how the gaze of the observer glides over the surface of the canvas along a vector indicated by the pointing index finger of the demonstrator's hand. Its objective is to reach the designated object, often the Virgin and Child or the body of Christ. In the quattrocento the vector, along with its designatum, was usually located on the surface, as it were. But exceptional variations on the gesture of demonstration arose in the baroque period. Thus a demonstrator portrayed by Philippe de Champaigne points inward, in an orthogonal direction in respect to the surface of the canvas. It was during this same period that penetrating through doors with one's gaze became a general feature in painting, and especially in seventeenth-century Dutch realism.

A door is also a *limen*, a "threshold." This Latin term brings us to the concept of liminality, which was first defined in 1909 by Arnold Van Gennep, the founder of French ethnology,[1] and was further developed by Victor Turner and other ethnologists.[2] Liminality plays a central role in the analysis of rites of passage. Can this concept be transposed to the field of painting and literature? In other words, do painting and literature have passage rite aspects? That is one of the questions to be dealt with in this chapter.

But doors in paintings are not only gaze-directing devices and *limina*. They are also signs, and as such they fall within the province of semiotics. Can doors be submitted profitably to the somewhat Procrustean bed of semiotic classification? That is another question the present chapter will endeavor to answer.

The Corpus

A number of studies in the past few decades have been written on paintings that contain doors, often within the context of what art historians call "the picture within the picture."[3] From one such study, André Chastel's "La figure dans l'encadrement de la porte" ("The figure on the threshold"), I have decided to appropriate part of my corpus.[4] The paintings I have thus appropriated are the *Adoration of the Magi* by an anonymous Flemish painter of the sixteenth century; *Mother near a Cradle* by Pieter de Hooch, circa 1659; and the *Meninas* by Velasquez, which is at the Prado Museum in Madrid.

To this group I have added eight other pictures: *Vanitas with Death on the Threshold* (also called *Death and the Courtier*), attributed to Pedro de Camprobin, circa 1630; *Nativity of the Virgin* by the anonymous Master of the Observance, circa 1440; the *Birth of Saint John* by Lucas Signorelli, circa 1598; the *Annunciation* triptych by the Master of Flemalle, circa 1498; *Young Woman Asleep* by Vermeer, circa 1660; the *Courtyard of a House in Delft* by Pieter de Hooch, 1658; and the *Babooshes* by an anonymous Dutch painter who belonged to the realistic current of the seventeenth century along with De Hooch, Molenaer, and other Dutch painters.[5]

I have also included a painting in which no door is visible but which is relevant for an exploration of the door motif in painting: the famous *Ambassadors* by Holbein the Younger. It is found as an illustration in the last chapter.

Although the corpus stretches over more than three centuries, I will not study it diachronically but synchronically, in the proper semiotic or structuralist spirit. That is to say, I will not examine the possible evolution of the door motif through the ages, nor discourse on the possible meaning of its evolution. What interests me here is the use of the door as a sign within the syntax of visual narrative.

Doors as Signs

Since doors in paintings are explicit signs of passage, it is proper to apply a theory of signs to analyze them. I have chosen the semiotic system elaborated by the French semiotician Algirdas Julien Greimas. Greimas constructed a model, the semiotic square,[6] which defined four modalities of possible actions in narratives: to want to, to have to, to be able to, to know how to do (*vouloir, devoir, pouvoir, savoir faire*). In other words, a narrative, be it verbal or visual, always describes an action (whatever it may be) in terms of the four modalities of wanting to, having to, being able to, or knowing how to do something, or in terms of their possible combinations, such as wanting to be able to (*vouloir pouvoir*) or being able to know how to (*pouvoir savoir*).

Greimas further organized these four possibilities along the diagonal, horizontal, and vertical lines of the logic square of medieval dialectics.[7] The semiotic square in figure III.1 organizes the narrative modalities of "to be able to do" along the diagonal lines of the contradictory axes, the horizontal lines of the contrary poles, and the vertical lines of the implied elements in

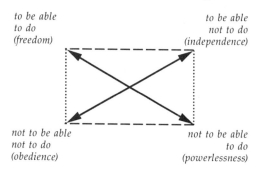

III.1 The semiotic square "to be able to do."
Diagram by the author.

the logical combination. Thus we have "to be able to do" (freedom), "to be able not to do" (independence), "not to be able not to do" (obedience), and "not to be able to do" (powerlessness).

Transposing this scheme to the syntax of the door-sign in painting, I shall first relate this semiotic square to the possibilities of actual passage on the part of characters represented in a painting, in the most concrete sense of "to be able to pass" physically from one space into another. I shall then analyze the cognitive, or seeing, modalities of passage; that is, "to be able to know to pass." The articulation of these modalities constitutes figurative representation.

Passage Modalities of Characters

Let us begin with the "not to be able to pass" (powerlessness) modality. In the cradle painting by De Hooch, the little girl looking out the door with her back to mother and cradle is certainly able to see what is going on outside the room but is not yet permitted to cross the threshold (fig. III.2). Similarly, the woman on the left in De Hooch's painting of a courtyard in Delft seems to stand frozen ("not to be able to pass") in the light coming through the door from outside, unlike the woman and little girl in the same painting, who are "able to pass" (freedom modality) into the courtyard (fig. III.3).

In the *Birth of Saint John* a spectator on the threshold remains there as though transfixed. He "is not able to enter," as though a divine power emanating from the infant and represented by the light is keeping him still (fig. III.4). In the *Adoration of the Magi* the armed men in the background through the doorway on the left, who block all passage ("not be to able to pass"), prefigure Herod's armed men who will later hunt for Jesus or the Roman soldiers of Pontius Pilate who will come to arrest him (fig. III.5). The figure of Death on the threshold in the *Vanitas* signifies the same "not to be able to pass" modality for the other character in the detail, the courtier (fig. III.6).

I see the obedience, or "not to be able not to pass," modality illustrated by the passage of the maid over the threshold in the *Nativity of the Virgin* (fig.

III.2 *Mother Near a Cradle* by Pieter de Hooch.
By permission of the Dahlem Museum, Berlin. Photo Jörg P. Anders.

III.7). It is the obedience not only of *dominis ancillae* but also of the spectator looking at the divine scene. This door signifies obedience in its highest sense: the impossibility of not passing through the door of faith.

More complex is the case of the character who stands at the threshold in the *Meninas* (fig. III.8). He is generally identified as the majordomo, or steward, of the queen of Spain.[8] One does not know whether he is ascending a flight of stairs leading out of the space in which the scene is being painted and casting a last glance over the threshold before actually leaving the room, or whether he is hesitating to enter the space in which stand the awesome presences of the king and queen. I classify the action of this man in relation to the door in the category of independence ("to be able not to pass"), though *hesitation* would be a more appropriate word to describe it. Similarly, I see the sleeping young woman in Vermeer's painting as an example of the same power "not to pass" through the door, but in a symbolic sense; she has already passed into the world of sleep, of dreams (fig. III.9).

If one orders the preceding interpretations according to the semiotic square, one obtains the disposition shown in figure III. 10. The drawback of

III.3 *Courtyard of a House in Delft* by Pieter de Hooch.
Photo National Gallery, London; by permission.

such an exact classification in four polar categories is, of course, that nuances cannot be taken into account. That is its Procrustean character. Every action tends to be seen either as a plus or a minus. There are no intermediary signs but only a somewhat excessive binarity. Still, such a classification is useful as a platform on which to rest our concept of liminality.

Cognitive Modalities of Characters

The passage modalities we have just examined in several characters are but isotopes—to use the terminology of Greimas—for the cognitive, or seeing, modalities of these same characters. In other words, the faculty each represented character has of passing or not passing through a door is but a double of a perhaps more important function; "passing through" also means "seeing through."

Thus in the *Vanitas* attributed to Pedro de Camprobin we have a character

III.4 *Birth of Saint John* by Luca Signorelli.
Photo Musées Nationaux, Paris; by permission.

who "is not able to see" Death on the threshold, although Death sees him.[9]
In De Hooch's cradle scene the little girl "is able to see" the world beyond
the threshold but "is not able to see" her mother, and her mother "is not
able to see" her. In the *Birth of Saint John* the same man who "is not able to
pass" the threshold "is able to see" the holiness of the child. Velasquez's
Meninas is a veritable encyclopedia of the possibilities of seeing and being
seen or not being seen, with its network of glances linking the characters
with each other, the painter with the characters, the king and queen with the
painter and with the characters through the agency of the mirror on the back
wall, and so forth.

In all these pictures, doors play a role of paramount importance in seeing.
They either permit the gaze of a specific character to connect with its object;
stand for the impossiblity of seeing what is represented; express the irresistible force of vision, the impossibility "not to see"; or signify the freedom of
seeing or refusing to see.

An especially interesting instance of the representation by a door of the
"being able to see" modality is the *Annunciation* by the Master of Flemalle
(fig. III.11). In this triptych, the half-open door—almost on the actual frame,
or at least on the represented limit (or *limen*) between the central panel and
the left panel—is a sign set there to show us how the kneeling donor "is able
to see" the miracle in the central panel. Although views of the actual world
are framed in all the doors and windows located at the back, none of the
characters in the picture sees this exterior world. As far as the trajectory of
gaze is concerned, the only thing that matters is the lateral opening of the
door between the panels. This is the only door that enables vision, rather
than mere seeing, to take place. The position of this door-sign tells us that
such vision is lateral in relation to the picture plane (just like the gesture of

III.5 *Adoration of the Magi* by an anonymous
Flemish painter, sixteenth century.
*By permission of Soprintendenza per i Beni
Artistici e Storici di Napoli. Photo Gabinetto
Fotografico Nazionale.*

demonstration in our quattrocento corpus in the preceding chapter); it is not
oriented toward the real world.

Once again I have arranged the various characters in my corpus, this time
according to the cognitive modalities on the semiotic square (fig. III.12).

Cognitive Modalities of Spectators

So far I have dealt exclusively with the function of doors in relation to
characters within the picture. Yet representational or figurative pictures have
more than a representational function that evokes identifiable objects in the
actual world—what Karl Bühler called the *Darstellungsfunktion der Sprache*
and Roman Jakobson called the referential function. Pursuing the linguistic
analogy, one could say that pictures, like literary texts, foreground one of
Bühler's three main functions of texts—expression/representation/

III.6 *Vanitas with Death on the Threshold,* also called *Death and the Courtier.* Attributed to Pedro de Camprobin.
By permission of the Hermandad de la Caridad, Seville.

appeal[10]—or one of the six main functions in the categorization of Jakobson.[11]

What interests us especially in this study is the appeal function—the conative one, in Jakobson's terminology. We have seen in the preceding chapter that some paintings are indeed structures of appeal (*Appelstrukturen*),[12] speaking to us and telling us things concerning our own performance. In a way, the corpus of paintings represented in this chapter is tantamount to a discourse about the seeing modalities of the observer. In the ultimate analysis, the visual arts always speak to us about seeing, about our cognitive capacities in relation to them, over and beyond what they may say as representations. Thus the passing and seeing isotopes I have briefly examined should be completed by an appeal isotope. Pictures speak to us about our capacity to see or not to see them through the signs (the doors, in this case) that the painters have set in them. But appeal itself is a sort of sign. It is, in fact, the very essence of what we defined in the preceding chapter as *ostentio.*

It may also be that doors in paintings are signs indicating that we the spectators are not only seeing but are being seen by the work of art. Doors are signs of the dialogic essence of art objects—to speak like Bakhtin. They speak to us about the dialectic of seeing, which always implies a being-seen relationship.

Here too the classification of Greimas may contribute something to a precise description of what it is to be the spectator of a picture. For instance, the terms *euphoria* and *dysphoria,* which he uses to express harmonic and non-

III.7 *Nativity of the Virgin* by the anonymous Master
of the Observance.
Photo Gabinetto Fotografico Nazionale; by permission.

harmonic relations between the text and the reader, may be borrowed with
profit.[13] If the seeing power of a character depicted in a painting corresponds
to the actual seeing of the outside observer, the relationship may be described as euphoric. Conversely, if the absence of seeing in a character (as,
for example, in the sleeping girl in the Vermeer painting) is opposed by a
seeing power on the part of the observer, the relation may be called
dysphoric.

Euphoric relations exist when the represented seeing power of the represented characters matches the actual seeing of the spectator looking at the
painting—that is, when both seemingly look in the same direction and with
the same intensity. Thus the little girl in the De Hooch painting with the
cradle and the woman standing alone at the threshold in the Delft courtyard
seem replicas of us spectators as we look at the picture planes. Their bodies
are parallel to ours, and they look at the rectangles forming the thresholds in

III.8 *Meninas* (detail) by Velasquez.
By permission of the Prado Museum, Madrid.

the same manner in which we look at the picture frames. These rectangles, even when they are not exactly parallel to the outlines of the picture frames, nevertheless seem to repeat them; they are isotopes of the pictures frames.

Euphoric relations of this kind seem to be characteristic of many realist paintings, not just of the De Hooch paintings in our corpus but also of the *Babooshes,* another paradigm of Dutch realism (fig. III.13). In the latter example, though, it is not a "live" character that stands as our replica but a character depicted in a picture within the picture hung on the back wall: a woman standing at a prie-dieu.

The Flemalle *Annunciation* triptych is a special case. The relationship between the seeing of the donor and our own seeing is euphoric; we too can see the scene on the central panel. But the gaze of the depicted character follows a lateral angle and thus crosses the orthogonal direction of our own gaze at a right angle. We were not meant to see someone who is actually looking at a real object but to watch someone who is having a vision.

In all these cases the doors are signs of the possibility of seeing, of pene-

III.9 *Young Woman Asleep* by Vermeer.
Diagram by the author.

trating directly the mystery of the mystic vision, not through a glass darkly
or *per speculum* but, as it were, through an open door.

Dysphoric relations exist when our power to see is not matched by a
similar capacity on the part of the depicted characters or when these characters are looking at us overtly or provocatively from inside the picture plane.
The latter case is typified by the demonstrators discussed in the preceding
chapter, and there is no need to expatiate upon the appeal function exercised
by their gaze.

Some paintings are based on dramatic irony, on the ignorance of the depicted characters versus the knowledge of the outside observer. Such is the
case in the *Vanitas.* Obviously the man in the painting does not know that
Death is standing in the door—but we know it is. In this case the door is a
vehicle of dysphoria because it allows the passage of a gaze that projects
outside the picture and is directionally antithetical to our own.

The *Meninas* is of special interest in this connection. Although it is a mon-
ument of baroque realism, no euphoric observer is represented in it. All the
gazes of the represented characters (except the girl standing close to the
painter) are directed orthogonally outward toward our own gaze. And yet

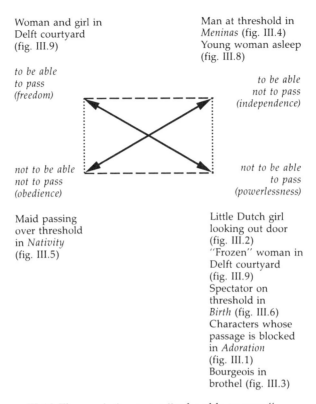

Woman and girl in
Delft courtyard
(fig. III.9)

Man at threshold in
Meninas (fig. III.4)
Young woman asleep
(fig. III.8)

to be able
to pass
(freedom)

to be able
not to pass
(independence)

not to be able
not to pass
(obedience)

not to be able
to pass
(powerlessness)

Maid passing
over threshold
in *Nativity*
(fig. III.5)

Little Dutch girl
looking out door
(fig. III.2)
"Frozen" woman in
Delft courtyard
(fig. III.9)
Spectator on
threshold in
Birth (fig. III.6)
Characters whose
passage is blocked
in *Adoration*
(fig. III.1)
Bourgeois in
brothel (fig. III.3)

III.10 The semiotic square "to be able to pass."

there is an implied euphoria in this painting: our gaze is none other than that of the king and queen who are reflected in the mirror. The painting may thus be said to represent the absolutism of seeing, just as the king and queen represent absolute power. To absolute power corresponds absolute seeing, and the spectator must look at the picture from the seat of the king to see it correctly. The whole painting seems to be about this parallelism of absolute power and absolute seeing—a gaze that survives even after absolute power has passed away.

Doors as Performatives

That doors can function as veritable guidelines for the penetration of the observer's gaze into a painting is obvious from the *Babooshes* and the *Young Woman Asleep* by Vermeer. In these paintings, as in many others, especially by Vermeer,[14] doors are veritable signals directed at us observers and ordering us to enter with our eyes. Reduplications of the more basic door which the frame of the picture essentially is, these doors are veritable perlocution-

III.11 *Annunciation* triptych by the Master of Flemalle.
By permission of the Cloisters, New York.

ary devices urging us to "Come in!" Our gaze thereby is directed in a sort of
orthogonal funnel going from foreground to background—the irresistible
movement described by Heinrich Wölfflin as a main characteristic of baroque pictures.[15]

Beyond this obvious perlocutionary effect, doors in paintings also have an
illocutionary, or perhaps a metapictorial, function: they tell us something
about painting itself. They tell us that they are dialogical objects and that
there is no such thing as one-sided observation of works of art; we are being
seen by the very object we are observing. Modern painters have often made
observations concerning this effect. Paul Klee wrote in his *Notebook*, "The
picture is watching us." In many respects, doors are signs of this illocutionary declaration performed by all great paintings: "I am watching you watching me." Doors are part of the dialectic seeing/being seen that is implicit in
all visual works of art. They are devices which make it manifest that art
objects are not objects placed on the canvas merely in order to be seen but
are also expressions of the seeing power of the artist, just as our gaze is not a
pure seeing but betrays our consciousness of a seeing presence within the
painting.

Doors as *Limina*

Not only are doors signs of the communication process between the art
object and the spectator; they are also autoreferent—that is, they point in the
direction of actual doors within society itself. They are signs of their own
symbolic functioning on the anthropological level. They are *limina*.

In Van Gennep's terminology, *liminality* is the middle term in the trilogical

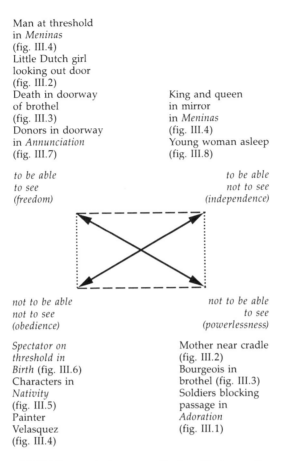

Man at threshold
in *Meninas*
(fig. III.4)
Little Dutch girl
looking out door
(fig. III.2)
Death in doorway
of brothel
(fig. III.3)
Donors in doorway
in *Annunciation*
(fig. III.7)

King and queen
in mirror
in *Meninas*
(fig. III.4)
Young woman asleep
(fig. III.8)

to be able
to see
(freedom)

to be able
not to see
(independence)

not to be able
not to see
(obedience)

not to be able
to see
(powerlessness)

Spectator on
threshold in
Birth (fig. III.6)
Characters in
Nativity
(fig. III.5)
Painter
Velasquez
(fig. III.4)

Mother near cradle
(fig. III.2)
Bourgeois in
brothel (fig. III.3)
Soldiers blocking
passage in
Adoration
(fig. III.1)

III.12 The semiotic square "to be able to see."

structure of rites of passage: separation/liminality/aggregation. *Passage,* for Van Gennep, means an actual movement over a threshold as well as a symbolic entering by a person into a new phase of life. Passage as liminality occurs physically when we enter a sanctified space, as in crossing the threshold of an actual temple or church—or even an art museum.

Van Gennep insisted on this physical aspect of passage. Following the American H. C. Trumbull,[16] Van Gennep set up a catalogue of actual passages, such as the taboo portico in the Greek and Roman polis, the bronze threshold in Greece, the monumental thresholds in Egypt and Assyro-Babylonia, and the private thresholds marked with signs of holiness in the Semitic world (the ritual caressing of a domestic god by Arabs, the kissing of the mezuza by Jews). In all of them, the important thing for Van Gennep was that crossing the threshold marked a separation from a context of normality and an entrance into a context of liminality. Returning to an-

III.13 *Babooshes.* Attributed to Hoogstraten.
Photo Musées Nationaux, Paris; by permission.

other normality, what Van Gennep called the aggregation, was also marked
by the crossing of a threshold, often the same threshold through which
separation had been effected.

To Van Gennep's list I would add others. Passage through the doors of the
medieval church, for example, was a visual passage: one had to experience
the visuality of the tympanum and its supporting walls and columns, which
often represented the Last Judgment. It was through all this visuality that
one entered the womb, the church itself.[17] In other words, one passed into a
liminal state, no longer in this life, not yet in the other—although, in respect
to visual decoration, one passed through a representation of that other state.
One's return to the actual world and normal life subsequent to the passage
out of the church into the street doubtlessly was impregnated with this
representation. Similarly, the passing of the faithful or the priest through the

mouth of the god in certain Maya temples was a physical entering of the god's architectural body through a door. These doors and thresholds were signs of the essential liminality of sacred space.

Can the concept of physical liminality be transposed to the field of aesthetics? If so, doors would be signs of the liminality not just of sacred space but also of aesthetic space. Represented characters in a painting would be caught between two doors—the one at the back of the depicted room and the frame-door through which our gaze enters. But representation itself could also be said to be liminal and caught between two doors.

The anthropologist Victor Turner described liminality as a "betwixt and between" space.[18] Using that terminology, not only are the liminal characters in a painting—the bourgeois in the brothel, for instance—betwixt and between; the process of representation and of aesthetic contemplation itself is designated as a betwixt and between space.

It is this idea—that representation is nothing but the ephemeral euphoric parallelism of gazes or the dysphoric crisscrossing of antagonistic glances within the locus of the painting—that is transmitted by door paintings. Certainly it is the essential message of a painting such as the *Meninas*. We have seen that in this picture the door at the back frames a disappearing (or ephemerally appearing) protagonist. This door does not merely echo the picture frame, the actual door of our regard, or the represented frame of the canvas on its stretcher painted by Velasquez. It also echoes, repeats, the frame of the represented mirror which retains the glances of the king and queen as though frozen in crystal. And this mirror itself echoes another mirror: an invisible but huge looking glass that must have stood confronting the whole scene, without which the *Meninas* could not have been painted.[19] *Frozen* is the operative word here. What we have is a freeze in the modern cinematographic sense. Like a freeze, the *Meninas* presents a liminal situation, a betwixt and between in the midst of the continuous movement of our eyes and fovea.[20]

The *Meninas* is about the liminal situation represented by the concept of posing for a painter; that too is a freeze of motion in the midst of life. The painting is also about the instant of creation, artistic creation, which is also a liminal instant, placed between the painter's glance at the posing characters and the touch of his brush on the canvas. Moreover, the *Meninas* is about painting as liminal death-giving through the glance of the painter: he freezes his actors in a pose and then freezes their life, their own regard, on the canvas for eternity.

In the *Meninas*, doors are an absolutely necessary ingredient. Without the isotopic relationship between the huge absent mirror and the ultimate door at the back of the picture, the idea of liminality could not have been represented; no description of art as a momentary death-giving could have been possible. In this painting—as in almost all the others I have introduced here, in particular the Dutch paintings—the liminality of doors is but the sign of the essential liminality of artistic gaze.

Such a statement about liminality is also made implicitly by the painting I have included in this corpus although no doors are actually represented in it: Holbein's *Ambassadors* (see fig. XII.3). The oblong blob that lies diagonally on the floor between the feet of the two depicted ambassadors was recognized from the beginning as an anamorphic representation of a human skull.[21] It is commonly accepted by art historians that the picture was to be hung beside a door so that a spectator who was about to cross the threshold might direct his glance slantwise across the canvas, thereby perceiving the skull. In perceiving the skull, however, the spectator was not only reconstituting the object deformed by perspective distortion; he was also veritably casting a glance of death at the picture, a glance that revealed to him that death was the truth of representation. This was tantamount to giving its correct name to the glance of the artist who freezes men into art objects. Yet in order to cast such a glance at art and representation, the spectator had to pass physically through a door and perhaps to freeze for an instant on the threshold. Passing through the door in order to find the secret of representation prefigures the ultimate passing of life through the threshold of death, when we finally reconstitute the temporal anamorphosis of our past, our life immensely stretched like a canvas or skin waiting for the proper perspective to reveal its true configuration.

It may be fit to observe here that the *Ambassadors* no longer hangs beside a door in a private home but on the wall of a house which is itself a sort of huge *limen:* a museum.

Museums as *Limina*

As we have seen, doors represented in paintings have an iconic relationship with the rectangular picture frames of the paintings which contain them; they resemble the frames as a rectangle resembles another rectangle. Yet these picture frames have an iconic relationship with actual doors—with the doors of the house which contains them, the museum.

The museum, too, is a betwixt and between, a fragment of liminal space inserted into the space of our normal everyday lives. In the terminology of Jean-Paul Sartre, the museum, like the pictures it contains, is the locus of a de-realization of everyday life. It is one of those places where the imaginative consciousness of the individual uses the world "as the negated foundation of the imaginary" and where the world "glides into nothingness."[22] In Sartre's terms, museums are places where "the gliding of the world into the bosom of nothingness" takes place perpetually in order for us to see "images." In other words, art is an absolute negation of reality and this negation is the very condition that permits us to see images of this reality. Seeing artistically is, indeed, a death-giving act in relation to everyday reality.

As Sartre explains apropos of a hypothetical portrait of Charles VIII,

As long as we observe the canvas and the frame for themselves the aesthetic object "Charles VIII" will not appear. It is not that it is hidden by the picture, but because it cannot present itself to a realizing consciousness. It will appear at the moment when consciousness, undergoing a radical change through which the world is negated, will itself become imaginative.[23]

This statement is corroborated by the behavior of people inside museums. They are inside the pictures as well as the museum, fascinated, absorbed. Often they do not see their fellow visitors but bump into them while stepping back to find the true vantage point and to better enter the image.

Veritable passage rites also take place at the entrances and exits of the museum. On entering, one must divest oneself of one's property and bags, and sometimes of one's coat. One views the sacred objects under the surveillance of a guard. One is sometimes guided by modern vestals and introduced by them into the mysteries of the collections. Information desks offer guidance and membership into the elite world of art. After the visit, aggregation into normal life is concomitant with a "realizing anew of reality," as Sartre would say. Yet it is a realization that occurs after we have given death, for a few minutes or hours, to reality.

In this respect, Holbein's *Ambassadors* is an allegory of aesthetic de-realization, not just of artistic creation. The contemplator of the skull image who returns to real life has seen and given death, has seen his own death as de-realization. He returns to real life having enhanced his negative potentialities, knowing that his power to see images is also a power to give death to the real world. In the final analysis, museum doors are much like the door beside which the *Ambassadors* was intended to be hung. Today, after almost two centuries of museum existence, doors in paintings are also signs of the liminal structure that contains them: the art museum.

Doors in Literature

Literary research has neglected a systematic approach to literature through semiotic studies of the object-signs it contains. To the best of my knowledge, only one article has tried to deal systematically with doors in fiction. Written by Thomas Sebeok and Harriet Margolis, it deals more with the illustrations for the books of Jules Verne and Conan Doyle than with textual descriptions of doors and windows.[24] Thus it may be rewarding to record systematically the passages in a novel in which doors and passages through doors occur and to see whether some sense can be made of their occurrence and recurrence.

Doors and windows occur constantly in Flaubert's *Madame Bovary*. From the very first page of the novel, when the new boy, Charles Bovary, crosses the threshold into the study hall, to the end, when the dying Emma hears through her open window the voice of a beggar singing the love song that had haunted her during her adulterous fling with Léon, almost every chapter begins with a door near which people or carriages stop and ends with a door or window that is being closed. The episode in which Charles first encounters Emma begins: "One night about eleven o'clock they [Charles and his first wife] were awakened by a noise: a horse had stopped at their door."[25] Later, "A young woman wearing a blue merino dress with three flounces came to the door of the house to greet Monsieur Bovary." It is Emma.

Windows are of special importance. During the famous ball scene, "Madame Bovary turned her head and saw peasants peering in from the garden, their faces pressed against the glass."[26] This triggers in Emma nostalgic reminiscences of her youth, of her happiness as a young girl on the farm; but, beyond that, the window serves as a sort of social comment: two worlds, two classes, come into visual contact through the window.

"One evening, when the window was open and she had been sitting beside it watching Lestiboudois the sacristan trim the boxwood, she suddenly heard the tolling of the Angelus. . . ."[27] "Madame Bovary had opened her window that gave on to the garden and was watching the clouds. . . ."[28] Many more chapters or passages within chapters begin like that. Even Emma's last lover, Léon, is associated with a window as he impatiently waits for the sound of her feet: "But still she didn't come. He took a chair and his eyes rested on a blue stained-glass window showing boatmen carrying baskets. He stared at it fixedly, counting the scales on the fish and the buttonholes in the doublets, his thoughts meanwhile roving in search of Emma."[29]

Are the doors and windows in *Madame Bovary* mere props, or do they tell a metaliterary tale concerning this novel of Flaubert, or concerning the genre of the novel itself? Doubtlessly, *Madame Bovary* can be described as a series of trajectories from door to door and through many doors by the protagonists of the novel. Flaubert seems to need an opening of a door in order to write a new chapter or describe a change in the mood of his heroine. The reason is perhaps to be found in his awareness that writing is a liminal process. Indeed, *Madame Bovary* is a representation of the liminal nature of fictional existence. The story of Emma is, as it were, caught between two doors, like the courtier in the Camprobin picture: the study hall door that ushers in the young Charles Bovary and the door of the gaping grave through which Charles watches Emma's coffin go down: "It went down and down. . . ."[30]

Doors are many and varied even in the titles of modern novels, from Gide's *La porte étroite* to Remarque's *Arch of Triumph* and Borchert's *Draussen von der Tuer*. Ordering all those doors according to their symbolism and functions would be an immense task. I would just like to conclude this short appendix on textual doors by taking a look at a story by Franz Kafka—a whole story about doors and the essential impossibility of passing through them. This story, "Before the Law," is also used as a sort of parable in *The Trial*.[31]

The story is told by a high priest at the Court of Law to make the hero, K, realize that he is deluding himself: "You are deluding yourself about the Court. . . . In the writings which preface the Law that particular delusion is described thus: before the Law stands a doorkeeper. To this doorkeeper there comes a man from the country who begs for admittance to the Law. But the doorkeeper says that he cannot admit the man at the moment. . . ." After the man has waited for some time, this doorkeeper says: "If you are strongly tempted, try to get in without my permission. But note that I am powerful. And I am only the lowest doorkeeper. From hall to hall, keepers stand at every door, one more powerful than the other. And the sight of the third man is already more than even I can stand."[32]

The end of the story is well known. The "man from the country" waits beside the first door until he becomes very old, slowly deteriorates, and dies. As he reaches his end, "the doorkeeper perceives that the man is nearing his end and his hearing is failing, so he bellows in his ear: 'No one but you could gain admittance through this door, since this door was intended for you. I am now going to shut it.' "[33]

One wonders whether the metaliterary dimension of this story is not the dominant one among all its possible dimensions, and whether Kafka did not intend the whole story to be an allegory of the reading of a great work of art by an audience, or by the average cultured hermeneutician. Indeed, entering such a work implies a sort of reading which becomes more and more difficult as one progresses into the text. This progress through a text always implies an ever greater de-realizing of the world in which we live and raises with ever greater intensity the question of existence—perhaps less our own existence than that of the work of fiction we are reading.[34] Yet it is a question that we perpetually leave aside, never trying to enter this door which designates fictional existence and its liminality. That actually means our never being really able to "penetrate" a text because then the illusion of fiction and art would no longer be effective. Fiction itself is the liminal—and vectorial—entering of a text through a door that is never designated by name.

In another chapter I observe how deeply rooted Kafka was in the Jewish tradition. "The man from the country" is really a translation of the Hebrew expression *amoretz*, designating the Jew who is not well versed in the Law, the Torah, the man who cannot read the texts.[35] We now understand more exactly what the guard was telling the man from the country. It is a story about the reading of books, about the reading of the Book, the Law. Through his description of the series of doors, the guard was causing the man from the country to have an in-depth glimpse of the whole text—a fantasy of penetrating the text through the whole series of doors. Beyond the merely literal stratum of the story, what was this guard, the first guard before the Law, really speaking about? Of nothing less than the terrible liminality of modern aesthetics, and of the terrible liminality of art.

IV

OPTICS IN EXTREMIS

We will see in later chapters to what extent the phantasm of the flayed body, cut up and opened to exhibit its internal mechanism, is linked to the intensity of the haptic vision of things, especially to the mannerist or expressionist vision. For German expressionism the objective was to recreate the mythic figure of the flayed Marsyas in a new type of beauty that would provide an explanation of the modern creative process through self-flaying, or self-alienation, and be capable at the same time of demolishing the old type of beauty *à la grecque*, the neoclassical "dumb" beauty of the harmonious human body.

The present chapter examines a type of expressionist phantasm that is antithetical to the haptic vision. It might be called the phantasm of the anorexic body because it projects the vision of a linear, filiform body, a human body as thin as thread or wire. Remaining faithful to the concepts of Riegl, I call this attitude optical. But the Wölfflinian term *linearity* might just as aptly render this concept. The optical reading of the body, like the haptic reading discussed in later chapters, was a feature of German expressionism. It was, in fact, common to all its branches: cinema, painting, literature.

As for cinema, there are a couple of classics of expressionist film whose optical images have remained etched in the collective memory since the films first appeared in the early twenties. Shots from these films have been perpetuated in monographs and in books about cinema history. A poster for the film *Wahnsinn* (Madness) by Conrad Veidt (fig. IV.1)[1] features a gesticulating, wirelike character very similar to a protagonist in Wiene's *Cabinet of Dr. Caligari*. The somnambulist Cesare, clad in black tights, committed a series of murders and rapes "as in sleep" before returning to the coffin in which his master, Dr. Caligari, kept him in a cataleptic state. The original poster for the film emphasized the living cadaver aspect of Cesare (fig. IV.2).

It is not the criminal personality of these madmen that interests me here but their bodily appearance, their apparent anorexia. This anorexia was a sort of common denominator of the expressionist body. It is quite evident in a group of figurines drawn by Franz Kafka (fig. IV.3). These figurines suggest a series of miniature Cesares.[2]

As I have shown elsewhere, these figurines must be placed in a global

IV.1 Poster for Conrad Veidt's *Madness.*
Author's collection.

expressionist context in which the human body is represented as a filiform skeleton.[3] Some cadaverlike self-portraits by Egon Schiele offer these same characteristics.[4] Even closer in appearance to Kafka's figurines are Kubin's rather protohuman forms (fig. IV.4).

The illustrations that Paul Klee made for the Kurt Wolff edition of Voltaire's *Candide*[5] look like those sticklike insects called phasms or phasmids.[6] The duelist by Klee (fig. IV.5) also looks much like the black duelist sketched by Kafka and reproduced at the top of figure IV.3.

What is the meaning of this skeleticism (if I may be pardoned a neologism)? What is the underlying signification of this anorexia in portraits, self-portraits, and fantastic creations of the time? A text of Kafka's perhaps contains the key to the mystery of this optics in extremis that renders the human body as a thin wire. An anorexic hero who appears prominently in one of Kafka's stories is the *Hungerkünstler*, the "hunger artist." Here is how Kafka describes his hero:

> The children stood open-mouthed, holding each other's hands for greater security, marveling at him as he sat there pallid in his black tights with his ribs sticking out so prominently, . . . answering questions with a courteous smile,

IV.2 Poster for *The Cabinet of Dr. Caligari.*
Photo Museum of Modern Art, New York;
by permission.

or perhaps stretching an arm through the bars so that one might feel how thin
he was.[7]

The impressario came forward . . . lifted his arms in the air above the artist, as
if inviting Heaven to look down upon its creature here in the straw, this
suffering martyr, which indeed he was, although in quite another sense;
grasped him round the emaciated waist, with exaggerated caution, so that the
frail condition he was in might be appreciated; and committed him to the care
of the blenching ladies, not without severely giving him a shaking so that his
legs and body tottered and swayed. The artist now submitted completely; his
head lolled on his breast . . . , his legs in a spasm of self-preservation clung
close to each other at the knees, yet scraped on the ground as if it were not
really solid ground.[8]

The essential aspect of the main character here is his puppetlike behavior,
quite similar to that of the black figurines in figure IV.3. The key Kafka gives
us is the character of the puppet, a character already inscribed in a tradition
that played a crucial role in the birth of German expressionism: German
romanticism. An essay on puppets by the romantic writer Heinrich von

IV.3 Black figurines drawn by Franz Kafka.
By permission of Schocken Books, New York.

Kleist, certainly one of the prominent figures in this tradition, reveals many hidden aspects of the expressionist homunculus. In this essay Kleist wrote of the puppet's noncorporeality:

> Thus, the point standing at the intersection between two lines (by the power of which it is projected toward the infinite) finds itself suddenly returning (toward us) on the reverse side; and, similarly, the image inscribed on the curved surface of the concave mirror—after stretching toward infinity—suddenly comes back toward us: it is in this very same manner that Grace reappears to our eyes (after Knowledge has stretched away toward the infinite) in order to show us that it exists at its highest degree only in the body that is the purest—that is, in a body that is not human at all or, on the contrary, in one that is made only of pure consciousness, that is, without any corporeal substance: in other words, in the Puppet or in God.[9]

Kleist himself was a somewhat pathological—perhaps anorexic—character, and his essay may reflect very personal problems. However that may be, the core of the essay is the idea that the puppet is more flexible, more graceful, and paradoxically more human than the human body. The essay is really about the paradox of the inversion in the relationship between nature

IV.4 *Chamois Hunting* by Alfred Kubin.
Collection of the Wallraff Richartz Museum.
By permission of the Administration of the
Museums and Bibliotheken, Cologne.

and artifice in artistic creation. This topos was common throughout the eighteenth century; it was, in particular, the theme of Diderot's *Paradoxe sur le comédien* and Rousseau's *Lettres sur les spectacles*. But Kleist goes even further than Diderot or Rousseau in stretching the paradox of the naturalness of the artificial. For Diderot, the superlative artist is the one who does not identify with his role but always preserves aesthetic distance between himself and his part.[10] For Kleist, the superior artist or actor is the one who succeeds in shedding his human behavior and even his human form to attain a stage in which he is capable of moving like a puppet. As Kleist asserted, bodily grace reaches its apex in the puppet or in bodiless divinity.

Kleist hated the human body, human flesh, and the pleasures of the flesh. His sad end by his own hand may be seen to a large extent as a liberation from the weight and clumsiness of his hated body. Kafka, too, hated his own body, though it had little flesh or weight.[11] He himself was an anorexic figure of sorts, consumed inside by tuberculosis. Kafka's black figurines, like his narrative of the hunger artist, may be seen as an effort to introduce thinness, even anorexia, as a new type of beauty. That, of course, was self-persiflage; Kafka's thin men are signs of self-torture.

But the anorexia was not a phantasm of Kafka's "sick" imagination. In the second half of the nineteenth century there existed a form of popular enter-

IV.5 *Il le perce d'outre en outre* by Paul Klee (1917).
*Museum of Art, Bern. By permission of the Klee Foundation,
Bern. Copyright 1989 by Cosmopress, Geneva.*

tainment based on anorexia, or at least on professional fasting. Forgotten for
decades, this peculiar practice was uncovered a few years ago by the Kafka
scholar Breon Mitchell.[12] There was, it seems, a whole group—almost a corporation—of persons who made a living by fasting. That paradox in itself
must have elicited Kafka's mirth. These hunger artists had their hour of
fame; their exploits were reported in the world press. They were also objects
of interest for physiologists and medical researchers. Even the term *hunger
artist* was not a product of Kafka's imagination, as was believed, I suppose,
by most Kafka scholars before the publication of Mitchell's study.[13] The term
was probably gleaned by Kafka from books or articles of the day, some of
them scientific studies on fasting.[14]

One professional faster, Giovanni Bucci, became a sort of champion of the
art in 1888 by fasting in Florence for one whole month "under true scientific
observation."[15] He took up a position inside a huge barrel in a covered
marketplace and received every day a number of visitors, with whom he
engaged in long conversations and bandied jokes. Another artist of this kind
was Claude Ambroise Seurat, styled "the living skeleton" (fig. IV.6), who
signed a contract according to which he had to appear in a show six times a
day, crawling on his arms and legs around a stage while allowing spectators
to seize him now and then by his waist to get the feel of his extreme emacia-
tion. Mitchell felt that Kafka probably borrowed some of his ideas from the
experiences of both Bucci and Seurat.

It matters little for my purposes whether Kafka did or did not invent the
term *Hungerkünstler*. What does matter is that he knew how to integrate this
bizarre self-torture into an allegory—or rather an etiology—of artistic creation. Did Kafka not declare in a letter to Milena Jesenka that "I am only
preoccupied with torturing and being tortured"?[16]

One question, however, must be answered: why did Kafka, after already
having chosen the self-flaying officer as a paradigm of the artist and profes-

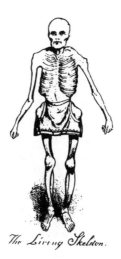

IV.6 "The Living Skeleton," Claude Seurat.
Illustration by Robert Cruickshank, 1826.

sional writer (see chap. IX), now choose the hunger artist? No doubt one must see at the root of this decision the will to self-representation; Kafka himself, by virtue of his tubercular body, was a hunger artist. This decision has perhaps a truly anorexic core in Kafka's wish to show his father the spectacle of his body: "See what you have done to me!"

But there is another possibility, having to do with the cultural background of the writer. Kafka belonged to more than one tradition. In his cultural roots the German romantic and expressionist tradition coexisted with the Jewish tradition. Beyond strictly theological considerations, his belonging to this second tradition may have engendered a specific view of language and textuality in general.

In terms of the central dichotomy around which I have organized this book, Judaism means essentially a tendency to see the textual as optic rather than haptic. There is at the core of the esoteric Jewish tradition—the cabalistic tradition rooted in the Zohar and the Haggadah—the idea that man has the shape of a letter, indeed *is* a letter or a combination of letters. Converseley, this tradition claims that the letters—the Hebrew letters in which the sacred text is written—*are* men. In one Jewish legend they are the "workers" who constructed the sacred text, the Bible. It was through the writing of the Bible, through the textual description of the world—that is, through the agency of the "working" letters—that God created this world. Another legend tells how the letters of the Hebrew alphabet presented themselves before God to offer their services in order to "write the world." But writing the world was tantamount to writing the Torah, since the writing of the holy book was concomitant with creation of the physical world that it apparently described.[17]

IV.7 Cabalist drawing of the tetragrammaton
YHVH as an anthropomorphic figure.
From Warren Kenton, *Kabbalah: Tradition of
Hidden Knowledge* (1979). *By permission of
Warren Kenton and Thames and Hudson, London.*

A "montage" of Hebrew letters placed on top of one another by seventeenth-century cabalists shows "the shape of God," that is, the shape of the anagram which represents God: YHVH (fig. IV.7).[18] It is not a drawing of a human shape; indeed, drawing the human figure or the divinity is strictly forbidden in the Jewish religion. It is rather a written representation of the Hebrew word *tselem*, which is translated "image" in the sentence "God made man in his image." Thus this combination of letters is really a text.

In constructing human figures with letters, the cabalists could claim that they were not "drawing" shapes but were only "writing." Such subterfuge probably accounts for the origin of Hebrew (and Islamic) pictograms.[19] An "artist" could replicate human shapes or the shapes of living animals provided it was done with letters. For the cabalists, this meant that the common denominator between man and God was the written language.[20] Thus Hebrew letters are the body of man, but they are also the body of God (in the sense of a noniconic anagram).

Kafka was not alone in playing this game with human letters. Klee drew pictures based on cabalistic letters, including *Mr. Z, X-chen,* and *Manhandling: A Pushes, A and M Fall Down while Pushing Each Other, P Is Hurled to the Ground.*[21] Still another is entitled *W Gruppe.*[22] There was also a Christian neocabalist tradition,[23] and it may be assumed that the sixteenth-century German mannerist Peter Flötner was inspired by this tradition when he drew his human alphabet (fig. IV.8).

IV.8 Anthropomorphic alphabet by Peter Flötner.
Photo The Albertina, Vienna; by permission.

In a way, Kafka and Klee are part of the relay in the Jewish and Christian cabalistic tradition's trajectory toward the creations of modern art. The graphic work of such artists as Henri Michaux, Max Ernst, and, more recently, Dotremont in France are based on the creation of semihuman, semihieroglyphic characters (fig. IV.9).

Let us look from this perspective at Kafka's little black figurines in figure IV.3. Many of them seem to be letters; indeed, their shapes seem to be so many variations on the letter K:

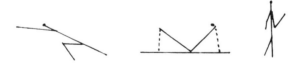

All these wiry little figurines may well be hunger artists. Even as possible representations of specific characters in Kafka's novels and stories, these silhouettes remain letterlike. We can see in them the dichotomy man/letter engaged in a duel to the death, or standing in the dock in front of the judges, or leaning against a blackboard in front of a class, or bent in a state of utter dejection, limbs metamorphosed into phasmid claws.

This letter K also has significance, of course, on a personal level. K is the initial letter of Kafka, the father's name. Moreover, K occurs not once but twice in this name, just as the letter H occurs twice in the divine anagram YHVH. Kafka was certainly conscious of this parallelism; it is not by chance that the letter K stands for the name of his protagonist in several stories and novels. (Even the name Samsa, the hero of *The Metamorphosis*, shows a consonantal parallel to Kafka.) That Kafka could not bring himself to write down the name of the father in full might even be seen as a neurotic symptom.

IV.9 Anthropomorphic script by Henri Michaux,
Mouvements.
By permission of Editions Gallimard, Paris.

If the names of the protagonists in Kafka's works have the status of anagrams, it is because of a superior parallelism with yHvH. In Kafka's interpretation, "Thou shalt not make images" has become "Thou shalt create only
anagrams." That is why, for Kafka, man can be only a letter, a sign; and that
is why the hunger artist has only a minimal sort of body, a letterlike
skeleton.

Lukács rightly termed Kafka one of the main literary representatives of
"modern religious atheism" (or "modern atheistic religion").[24] What Lukács
was alluding to is related to the hidden, *deus absconditus* character of Kafka's
actual father. Through his signlike anorexic figures and letter heroes Kafka is
making a double statement: (1) because you believers do not really have a
god but only a sign of it, an anagram, I do not have a real father, and (2)
because I do not have a real father, because my own father is hidden, absent,
a mere letter, you believers cannot see your god and perhaps do not have a
god at all but only an anagram of it.

The first proposition is a scream of personal despair camouflaged as a
rationalization of the sign character of the hidden god. The second is a
rationalization of the absence of God as a reflection of Kafka's own creative
situation as a writer; it is a metaliterary discourse whose content is that signs,
and especially the compound of signs that is literature, do not refer the
reader to any transcendent meaning. The letters, in ultimate analysis, are
signs that refer only to themselves, not to any transcendental reality.

"Man as a letter" had all-encompassing implications for Kafka. The letter-

IV.10 *The Way to the City Castle* by Paul Klee.
*By permission of the Klee Foundation, Bern, and
Cosmopress, Geneva.*

like body of the protagonist was also a sign of the dominant linearity of the
narrative itself. Indeed, Kafka's narratives are on the side of linearity, or
optics, rather than haptics. It is important that the K who is the hero of *The
Castle* is a land surveyor; it means that his activity is essentially vectorial, the
measuring of fields and landed property in terms of width and length. K
moves like a vector or index in those two dimensions; he almost never
moves in the more haptic dimension of depth.

We have seen that there is a Klee–Kafka connection that has never been
seriously explored. In its vectorial aspect Kafka's novel also suggests a series
of pictures by Klee in which "arrows" seem to move laterally in the essential
flatness of the pictures. One of these drawings, *The Way to the City Castle*,
may be considered an almost exact parallel to what Kafka sought to achieve
in *The Castle* (fig. IV.10). In that novel, as well as in other stories, Kafka dealt
with the impossibility of moving in depth toward a goal; the only possible
move was lateral, without ever reaching a goal. In "The Next Village" and
"Description of a Struggle," for example, no goals are reached and no struggle actually takes place.

A similar linearity in expressionist films probably accounts for the over-
whelming presence in them of anorexic heroes. *The Cabinet of Dr. Caligari*
and *Wahnsinn* both are vectorial, foregrounding gesture: the running about
of hero and criminal who look for unattainable or nonexistent goals.[25] Both
films contain a theory of reading films that is essentially optical. In *Caligari*
the spectator is first "told" to follow the winding path of Cesare through the
town, over the roofs, into the bedroom where the girl is sleeping; subsequently, the spectator is compelled to visually follow the path of Cesare to

the mental hospital where "Caligari" is hiding. The whole film might be described as a series of linear trajectories that are also trajectories for the eyes of the spectator to follow. Like K in *The Castle,* the protagonist of *Caligari* goes nowhere and reaches no goal. What is left for us to see in these works is a sui generis vectoriality. It is the same vectoriality that is described by Klee in *The Way to the City Castle.* The vectors, of course, lead us nowhere, just as following K in his peregrinations would lead us nowhere near the castle.

The concept of optic reading thus can legitimately be extended to expressionist cinema. German expressionist movies seem to be characterized by the omnipresence of winding paths or corridors that compel the eye to follow them. In this they diverge from Soviet cinema, which is based instead on cuts and montage, the real flesh or skin of celluloid film; cutting and pasting are procedures that deal with epidermic operations.

And it can be no surprise, surely, that the first heroes of the American *roman noir*—the heirs, in many respects, of the expressionist heroes—were thin men. I am referring specifically, of course, to Dashiell Hammett's novel *The Thin Man.* Yet even before Hammett's mysterious and actually nonexistent thin man appeared on the scene,[26] in the late thirties, Hammett invented an anorexic, almost self-flagellating hero, Ned Beaumont, the protagonist of *The Glass Key.*[27] He is flat-chested and hollow-cheeked, not unlike Kafka's black puppets. When he is hit by the fists of the hoodlums against whom he is pitted, one of them "scooped up Ned Beaumont's legs and tumbled them on the bed. He leaned over Ned Beaumont, his hands busy over his body. Ned Beaumont's body and arms jerked convulsively and three times he groaned. After that he lay still."[28]

A more recent development on this theme is found in the science fiction novel *The Shrinking Man* by Richard Matheson, in which the body of the protagonist diminishes more and more as a physical entity until it reaches the dimensions of a molecule, then of an atom, and vanishes in the solitude and freedom of infinitesimal space. To the modern anorexic hero, the silence of infinite space, which for Pascal meant *horror vacui,* is a synonym for freedom.

V

TOEING THE LINE

Ostensibly, the theme of the short story "Linija i tsvet" (Line and color) by Isaac Babel, published in 1923, is a meeting of the author in prerevolutionary days with Kerenski, who was to lead the February Revolution in Russia. This was the democratic revolution that did away with the tsarist regime in 1917, a few months before being liquidated in turn by Lenin's Bolshevik Revolution, the October Revolution. Although Babel's purpose appears to be to create comedy rather than to urge ideological commitment, his narration of this humorous anecdote, which makes Kerenski appear pompous and ludicrous, is quite compatible with Babel's own *engagement* and shows that his intention was primarily political. Nevertheless, a few symbolic motifs that intertwine to form the story constitute an underlying network of reflections on politics in terms of a set of relations in the visual field, and it is this set of relations I intend to analyze here.

Before proceeding with the analysis, however, let us hear the voice of the toposensitive Babel as he tells us about his encounter with the shortsighted Kerenski in a sanatorium at Olila in Finland.[1]

> I met Aleksandr Feodorovich Kerenski for the first time on the twenty-first of December 1916 in the dining room of the Olila sanatorium. It was Zatsarenyi, a lawyer from Turkestan, who introduced us to each other. Concerning this man Zatsarenyi I knew that he had had himself circumcised at the age of forty. The grand duke Peter Nicolayevich—an unbalanced character who had fallen into disfavor and had been sent into exile in Tashkent—set great store by Zatsarenyi's friendship.
>
> This grand duke used to run around in his birthday suit through the streets of Tashkent; he had married a Cossack woman and would light candles in front of a portrait of Voltaire as though it were an icon representing Christ; he had ordered the draining of the immense Amu-Daria plains. Zatsarenyi was his friend.
>
> So, we found ourselves all together in Olila. Ten kilometers away glistened the great blue granite cliffs of Helsinki. . . .
>
> The dining room smelled of pine wood, of the fleshy bosom of Countess Tyszkiewicz, and of the silken underclothes of British officers.
>
> At the table, a converted Jew from the police department, a very polite person, was seated beside Kerenski . . . Countess Tyszkiewicz [was as] beauti-

ful as Marie Antoinette . . . Kerenski ate three cakes and left with me for an outing in the forest. Fröken Kirsti brushed past us on her skis.

"Who is that?" Aleksandr Feodorovich asked.

"Old Johannes," I answered. "He is bringing back some brandy and some fruit from Helsinki. Do you remember coachman Johannes?"

"I know everybody here," Kerenski answered, "but I cannot see them."

"Are you shortsighted, Aleksandr Feodorovich?"

"That is right: shortsighted."

"Then you must wear spectacles, Aleksandr Feodorovich!"

"Never."

I exclaimed with youthful vehemence: "Look here, you are not only blind, you are almost dead! Line, divine outline, the master of the universe, has slipped away from you forever. We are walking here together in an enchanted garden in the splendor of this indescribable Finnish forest. Until our last day, we will never see something more beautiful. But you cannot see the frozen pink banks of the waterfall, right here, near the river. This weeping willow tree leaning over the waterfall: you are incapable of seeing its Japanese chiseling. The red trunks of the pine trees are covered with a layer of granulous and sparkling snow which begins with an immaculate line at its point of contact with the tree, an undulating line as though traced by Leonardo. It is crowned by the reflection of flamboyant clouds. And what about the silk stocking of Fröken Kirsti and the line of her voluptuous leg? Buy some spectacles! Aleksandr Feodorovich, I beg you!"

"Child," he answered, "do not waste your time. The fifty kopeks that the glasses would cost me are the only fifty kopeks I will ever save. I do not need your line, which is sordid like reality. You do not live better than a trigonometry teacher, whereas I am surrounded with wonders. What do I care about seeing the freckles on the face of Fröken Kirsti when, by virtue of my negative capacity of not being able to make her out in full detail, I can imagine what I want to imagine? What do I care about clouds in the Finnish sky when I see a tumultuous ocean above my very head? The whole world is for me an immense theater in which I am the only spectator without spectacles. The orchestra is playing the overture for the third act, the stage is far away from me as in a dream, my heart swells with excitement, I see the purple velvet of Juliet's dress, Romeo's lilac silk, and cannot see any false beards—and you would like to blind me with your fifty-kopek spectacles?". . .

I saw Aleksandr Feodorovich again six months later, in June 1917, when he had become the supreme commander of the armies of Russia and the master of our destinies.

On that day, the Trinity bridge had been raised.[2] The Putilov workers were marching on the Arsenal. Tramcars lay on their sides like so many dead horses. A meeting was taking place in the House of the People. Aleksandr Feodorovich delivered a speech about Russia, Mother and Spouse. The crowd was crushing him under its animal passion. What did he imagine he could see in that swelling, bristling herd? He, the only spectator without spectacles? I do not know.[3] But after him, Trotsky stepped onto the podium, twisted his mouth, and began, in a voice that did not leave any hope: "Comrades and brothers. . . ."

We are offered an antithetical set of possibilities: "line, divine outline, the master of the universe," or "line, which is sordid like reality," the first asserted by the narrator, the second Kerenski's reply.[4] I assume that the first proposition, which is prolinear, is genuinely Babel's. The second stance, antilinear, is Kerenski's as Babel saw it.

On first reading, the story certainly seems to be a political allegory. Babel sets the vagueness and haziness of Kerenski's vision against the razorlike sharpness of the Bolshevik line represented by Trotsky. Actually, a whole political-artistic symbolism is implicit in his choice of the term *line*.[5] It was the Russian Revolution that introduced *linija*, in the sense of "political direction" or "program," into the vocabulary of politics. The role of the Communist party, it was said then in the official propaganda sheets, was primarily to "set a line" for the rest of the country to follow. And it was in the early postrevolutionary period that Sergei Eisenstein made his great film *The General Line*. Eisenstein's film, as well as political posters, represented this line as a great furrow drawn on the Russian plains by the plows in the first collective fields. The line was also the thin yellow stripe on the horizon of revolutionary posters, a harbinger of the sun about to rise on the "singing morrows" of the Communist future.[6] And it was the line represented by troop-carrying trains stretching across the Russian *chernozie*; didn't Lenin say that "revolutions are the locomotives of history"?

Yet the line was also merciless; like Trotsky's voice, it "did not leave any hope." Indeed, the successful revolutionaries introduced the concept of "toeing" the party line and of "deviating" from it. The concept of political deviation probably stems from the writings of Lenin.

Against this merciless line, the bourgeois democrats such as Kerenski offered only vague promises and a vague vision of a heterogeneous society made up of pressure groups and classes juxtaposed haphazardly, without a strict linear (ideological) framework to hold them together. Their perception of the political scene was hazy. Whereas Lenin saw the social landscape of Russia as class pitted against class in razor-sharp antagonism—the proletariat against the bourgeoisie, the peasants against the kulaks, and so on—Kerenski saw a mosaic of groups coexisting, an impressionistic concatenation held together by a national mystique of Mother Russia. As Kerenski told Babel, "That is right: shortsighted."

It is difficult to believe that Babel, the Red Cavalry war correspondent, was interested in the avant-garde aesthetic currents of his time as well as its politics. And yet his own very special optical–haptical dichotomy presented in this story corresponds not only to a conflict between political ideologies but also to a conflict between aesthetic viewpoints. Doubtlessly his contemporaries, the formalists and constructivists, also favored a "line" in matters of aesthetics. So did the exponents of montage in cinema, including Eisenstein and Pudovkin.[7] Montage is a doctrine of sharp, razorlike cuts and sharp juxtapositions, not of dissolves and superimpositions, which might be seen as filmic equivalents of Kerenski's vagueness.

Even before the revolution broke out, the constructivists had established the supremacy of their "line" in the visual arts. Malevitch had already spoken of art as the ability to construct "on the basis of weight, speed, and direction of movement" and had declared that "any carved-out pentagon or hexagon would [be] a greater work of sculpture than the Venus de Milo or David."[8] Indeed, one might claim that his movement, suprematism, was essentially an establishing of linear supremacy. In later years, Malevitch went so far as to write that

> we may make the analogy that human life is like a line on which we find various stages at which man's attitude to color changes, similar to the other line along which man passes all the various social conditions from the village to the capital. If we compare these two lines of life, we will probably come to identical conclusions, since each section on the line of progress toward the capital—village, neighboring town, country town—is the free growth of . . . cultural energy.[9]

In terms of Babel's "Linija i tsvet," the personal development of the great Russian painter Kandinsky is particularly interesting. Kandinsky's early works were impressionist or neoimpressionist in character. Even his programmatic and epoch-making 1912 book, *On the Spiritual in Art*, did not take a stand against impressionism but rather against realism and the prevailing symbolist movement (or its surrogate, art nouveau) insofar as this movement favored a narrative and anecdotal line and did not see "pure painting" as its ultimate objective.[10] Nevertheless, fourteen years later his second theoretical work, *Punkt und Linie zur Fläshe* (Point and line to surface), took a stand against impressionist techniques and favored the foregrounding of pure geometrical forms as a way to achieve great works of art.[11] He had done a complete about-face!

The distance between the first book and the second was the distance covered aesthetically by Kandinsky himself. This distance measured exactly the gap that separated color from line. Immediately after publishing *On the Spiritual in Art*, the painter had embarked on a nonfigurative type of painting, but it was a sort of nonfigurative painting that might have deserved the name impressionistic. It was certainly not based on the use of line but on colored stains as essential elements. This period of Kandinsky's work is usually called his "lyrical" period—a phrase that nicely expresses the fact that color and its effects, not linear or geometrical structures, were foregrounded by his technique.

What was the cause of his later abrupt change? Doubtlessly it was his encounter with postrevolutionary Russia. In 1918 Kandinsky left Germany for Russia, where constructivism was prevalent. The experience was decisive. It was during this visit that the painter published a veritable ode to line, actually named "O linii" (On line), in a study entitled "Little Articles on Big Questions."[12] Kandinsky shows us how, by virtue of the line, a text becomes a picture:

First, the short stroke, the tie or the hyphen -
Second, the long stroke, the dash ————

The reader, transformed into a spectator, gradually extracts first the outer expediency, then the practical meanings, from these signs; and then, on a new page, a clean sheet of paper, the reader suddenly obtains a new graphic sign:

———————————————————————————

a line. Kandinsky writes:

> The fate of line . . . requires a special description. . . . Line experiences many fates. Each creates a particular, specific world, from schematic imitation to unlimited expressivity. These worlds liberate line more and more from the instrument, leading to complete freedom of expression. . . . The graphic work that speaks by means of these forms belongs to the first sphere of graphic language—a language of harsh, sharp expressions devoid of resilience and complexity. . . .[13]

"A language of harsh, sharp expressions": one seems to hear the voice of Trotsky, "a voice that did not leave any hope." Did Babel know this study by Kandinsky? It is certainly probable that he read the national magazine that published the study, *Iskusstvo* (Art) in its new Bolskevik form.

When Kandinsky returned to Germany he was still a militantly nonfigurative artist but his style had changed: the impressionistic use of lyrical color stains had been discarded, and geometry and line had become all-important as structuring elements for his abstract compositions. He had taken his first step toward formulating the aesthetic doctrine that was to become a pillar of the new art school, the Bauhaus. Kandinsky's evolution clearly shows that the prevailing artistic direction went from impressionism to constructivism to the Bauhaus's "linear ideology."

Against this background, Babel's story takes on fuller dimensions. The story actually raises the question of parallelism (or nonparallelism) between political and aesthetic developments. It was Walter Benjamin who first addressed this question overtly, in a speech delivered at the Paris convention of antifascist writers in 1937. This scholar, a German Jew then living in exile in Paris, declared that fascism was "the aesthetization of politics." He had in mind, obviously, the Wagnerian aspect of Hitlerism, and perhaps the architecture of Albert Speer and others. To this aesthetization, Benjamin said, the only response must be "the politization of aesthetics." For Benjamin, communism was such a politization of aesthetics, and this politization implied the hegemony of "line."

As a model for this politization of art, Benjamin favored the work of his friend Bertolt Brecht. Brecht, too, was an admirer of line. Brechtian theater is dialectics on the stage, that is, the representation of a political development whereby a given situation reverses into its opposite, a given political line into an antithetical line. Linearity in Brecht was the linearity of this circle of dialectic transformation. Linearity was also vectorial; chapter II dealt at some length with the gesture of demonstration, which lies at the core of Brechtian aesthetics. This *Gestus des Zeigens,* this showing that one is showing, which turns the actor into an index of the part instead of an icon of it, encapsulates the concept of the politization of aesthetics. For the Brechtian, aesthetics must become globally vectorial and linear in the sense of presenting concrete models instead of suggesting some hazy or poetic reality.

Babel declared himself Brechtian even before Brecht. In 1923, in "Linija i tsvet," Babel indirectly proclaimed his adherence to the vectorial as an artistic principle. And indeed, most of his stories, like Brecht's plays, are demonstrations of some sort. In most of them the presence of the narrator is visible, foregrounded. We are invited to read "Linija i tsvet" as a demonstration. What is being demonstrated, of course, is that line and outline are all-important as aesthetic elements. Babel's story also contains an implicit theory for reading the world and its representation. We are being told that there is perhaps no essential difference between aesthetics and politics, that politics and aesthetics are but two sides of the same coin; aesthetics must be read in political terms and, conversely, politics must be read with an aesthetic eye. There is perhaps nothing new in the first part of the proposition; it is, after all, the basic tenet of socialist realism. But there is a great deal of originality in the second part of the proposition.

Babel's story also has its metaliterary aspect. It is a metadiscourse about reading itself, constituting a veritable theory of reading. One must read line and not color, it tells us. Such a conclusion is astonishing when one recalls that Babel's style has been termed impressionistic. Babel's reader must look for the line, the thread, that holds his stories together and not become captivated by the colors, the anecdotes.

In the year that followed the publication of Babel's story, Lenin died, Stalin was well on his way to absolute power, and Russia was regressing to an aesthetic for the masses, which meant a reintroduction of narrative content and figurative aesthetics onto the art scene. It was a regression toward the idea that art could only be political through its content, not through its style and technique. It also meant a discarding of line and pure geometry as basic elements in pictures and sculptures. The real avant-garde had to be eliminated.

Babel and other exponents of constructivism and formalism in the arts, including Malevitch, also had to be eliminated, in one way or another, as formalism fell victim to the sharpness of the line it had once exalted.

VI

HOMUNCULUS AS MAP

Studies of the physiology of the human cortex long ago discovered that the human body reproduces itself, as it were, on its own cortex, that there is self-representation on the cortex.[1] Thus the cortex contains a diagram of its own body image, but this imprint is a stunted and deformed homunculus. A classic drawing shows the physiognomy of this homunculus, with its huge hands, mouth, and eyes (fig. VI.1). As one sees, there are actually two homunculi, one relating to the sensory and the other to the motor aspects of the body. The hugeness of the hands, mouth, eyes, feet, and gustatory apparatus in relation to the other body parts and organs is due to the importance of these zones in terms of cortical activity and sensitivity.

From the standpoint of modern physiological-semiotic theory, such as that of Von Uexkuell, one might say that this homunculus represents the *Innenwelt*, the inwardly staged model of the actual body as *Umwelt*, as cognitive map of the world. Thus the homunculus would represent a cognitive map of a cognitive map.[2] The implications of the existence of such a creature within us, especially for artistic and literary creation and its aesthetic appreciation, are tremendous. This chapter and the next three examine some of these implications.

Just as the human cortex contains its own body image, just as "there is" this phenomenon of body representation within the human cortex, it may be claimed that ideology and discourse and their corresponding visual representations contain the vision of a distorted human body that is always present as a sort of watermark or algorithm located deep behind discourse itself. It is not a model in the sense in which Max Black uses the term—that is, it is not an imaginary construct that is noniconic in character and makes for a more accurate analysis of its complex correlative in so-called reality.[3] Rather, it is a built-in structure or map, albeit a distorted one. The reality of the body *qua representatio* is its essential distortion. Whereas the introduction of a model is tantamount to the introduction of a perspective change in language, the actual presence of a built-in map inside the cortex means that all body representation is done with reference to this inner body map.

In terms of heuristics, the presence of this homunculus produces a body which is not merely visual but which intersects and interconnects with ideo-

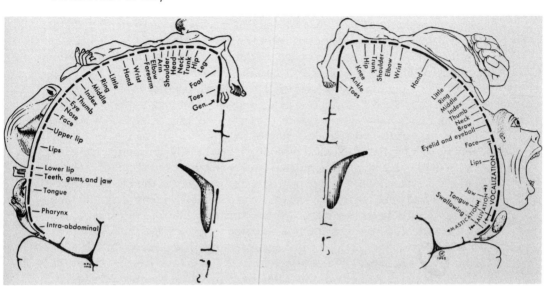

VI.1 The sensory and motor homunculi. From Wilder Penfield and
Theodor Rasmussen, *The Cerebral Cortex of Man,* figs. 18 and 19.
By permission of Macmillan, New York.

logical discourse. It actually is a body made of language; it reveals the ideological text as a sort of body pictogram, transforming any text into the body
it ultimately represents. The gain one makes by introducing such a model is
the production of meaning, which translation and perspective shifts always
bring about.

The recent concept of a political unconscious is also a map or structure. If
one must take that model seriously, as some philosophers assert,[4] one must
also take seriously the concept of a cortical homunculus. This homunculus
might indeed be one of the forms taken by this unconscious, a matrix for
representation or a representation-regulating module, a matrix where the
human body and the pictogram body of ideological discourse meet.

Another model that we may connect with our homunculus is that of Bakhtin. To the best of my knowledge, only Mikhail Bakhtin among twentieth-
century scholars has attempted to describe a body concealed behind political
discourse. His greatest contribution to historical research is probably his discovery that a huge and grotesque human body is situated in the hinterland
of discourse. It was this body which lurked behind the table talk of medieval
monks in the seclusion of their monasteries and loomed up behind the official speeches of prelates. Bakhtin located it in the world of Rabelais.[5] The
great Russian scholar doubtlessly saw Rabelais's creations, his giants
Grandgousier and Gargantua, as metaphors for the extended and omnipresent body.

Bakhtin's notion of this verbal presence of the obscene body can be extended to visual creations. A grotesque human body lurks behind many medieval sculptures and manuscript illuminations.[6] This same body, marked with the sign of the devil, later came to the fore as the central theme in the paintings of Hieronymus Bosch. It became even more visible in the overt distortions of political caricature; in the sixteenth-century broadsheets describing a topsy-turvy world, one gets glimpses of an inverted body as man walks on his hands and thinks with his feet. It became omnipresent behind the discourse of the French *sans culottes*.

It may well be that ideological discourse—not only historical discourse but also aesthetic and literary discourse—and ideological representation orient themselves, insofar as they represent themselves and/or the Other, according to this body map that is inscribed in the cortex. They may well take their bearings according to this map, this homunculus, that produces discourse. This homunculus may also provide the map according to which historical, aesthetic, and literary discourse becomes manifest. The presence of this body in the brain also means the presence in it of a symbolic political body: the body of the king, the body of the state, the body of the enemy, and so forth. But this body map, remember, is distorted. In its descriptions and representations it foregrounds now the hands, now the eyes or mouth, now the genitals of the represented characters. Representational activity in the cortex may similarly foreground and distort the represented body in discourse or in pictorial activity, according to the need of the moment.

What we might call the homunculus theory was anticipated by many artists. It became almost explicit when phrenology was so popular in the mid–nineteenth century. In France, for instance, one nineteenth-century draftsman actually did refer to a cortical map inside the brain of the person he was caricaturing. In 1870 A. Belloguet represented the brain of Pope Pius IX as containing (that is, as being obsessed with) naked women and gold coins (fig. VI.2).[7] According to the cartoon's title, the phrenological map inside the papal brain was worthy of the pillory.

At about the same time, another caricaturist, Alphonse Hector Colomb, who was also interested in phrenology, showed a head of Bismarck containing a little man, an acrobat walking upside down.[8] An exploration of European and American cartoons of the period would surely yield other little men inside the big heads of powerful men.[9]

In the past decade the ideas of the psychoanalyst Jacques Lacan concerning a mirror stage in human development have become fashionable. According to Lacan, the human being cannot become a self without the mediation of self-representation, that is, without an encounter and subsequent recognition between the human person and his or her body image in a mirror.[10] This idea doubtlessly represents an important development in the analytic conception of the human psyche. But Lacan seems to have been unaware of the existence of the homunculus built into the physiology of each human being. This cortical homunculus itself is a sort of deforming and distorting mirror in

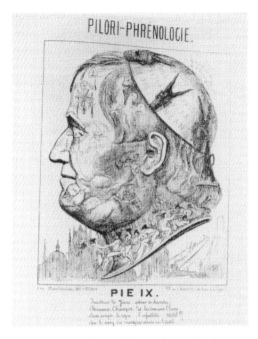

VI.2 Phrenology-Pillory, from *L'assiette au beurre.*
Author's collection.

respect to the body. It is, however, a mirror that does not distort the overall global structure of relations within the human body but only foregrounds specific parts according to a criterion one might call cortical toposensitivity. In respect to representation and the discourse of representation, this mirror is a little like the convex mirror of Parmigianino in which the hand of the painter who owns the mirror and is looking into it appears enormous in relation to the rest of his body.[11] And indeed one could easily claim that troubled times—the times of mannerism, expressionism, revolution—privilege the cortical vision over normal apperception.

Conversely, the existence of the cortical homunculus implies that specific theories of reading are built in as implicit structures of the brain. It is a fact that creative imagination reads; it reads pictures and texts, it reads the world, it reads the discourse of the Other. Yet, in order to do so it must also read its own internal homunculus.

Coming to the organizing theme of this book, one might say that haptics plays a central part in this reading. On one hand, the reading consists in a sort of haptic touching of the internal body image; on the other hand, representation consists in a projection of this internal reading and touching onto a painted figure or textual discourse. This is representation proper: the cortical homunculus is translated into a picture or a three-dimensional object, a piece of sculpture. In painting and drawing, an essentially three-dimensional map is externalized on the canvas. In sculpture the externalization is translated onto plastic volumes. A similar phenomenon is found on the textual level: textual body descriptions are but the projections as texts of intensive haptic depth readings. The description proper, the text, is only a surface phenomenon.

There have been, throughout the ages, attempts at depth writing and depth painting. One such attempt is described in chapter IX. We have also seen the presence of the haptically felt body through the centuries. Artists, philosophers, and authors had the intuition of this internal body that inhabits us. From ancient times onward, philosophically inclined cosmographers and cartographers created the tradition of the anthropomorphic map, the map shaped like a human body. This tradition and its textual implications are examined in chapter VII.

Over the course of time there were many other "translations" or projections of the homunculus. To trace further developments in these presentations, one would have to explore, first of all, the so-called organic tradition, which dates as far back as classical times. This tradition represented the king as the head of the nation and the various institutions of the kingdom as its organs and limbs.[12] A tradition diverging from the classical foregrounded one single part of the body. This was the Hobbesian tradition with its concept of the king as a sort of devouring stomach constituted by the digested bodies of his subjects. The body of this Leviathan-king was crystallized in an etching that served as the frontispiece of the first edition of Hobbes's *Commonwealth*.[13]

This latter tradition stemmed from sixteenth-century mannerism. The picture of Rudolf II as Vertumnus, the Roman god of spring, was well known. It was commissioned by Rudolf to Giuseppe Arcimboldo, the Milanese artist who frequently traveled to Rudolf's court. Arcimboldo represented the king as a conglomerate of all the fruit that gets its start in spring. In doing so he was following the precept set down by his friend Comanini, the philosopher, who was also patronized by Rudolf. "The duty of the painter," Comanini wrote, "is to reveal the face of the King that is hidden in all things."[14] Rudolf as Vertumnus is not far away from Leviathan in the Hobbesian conception and, in fact, may have inspired it. Both are composite images, with the essential difference that Vertumnus is constituted by the fruit he has digested, whereas the Leviathan is formed by human bodies. Hobbesian ideology thus may be regarded as a product of the philosophical aesthetics of mannerism, and the representation-directing homunculus may be said to have been translated by painters into the composite mannerist homunculus à la Arcimboldo.

In many respects, Hobbes's figure of the Leviathan, exposing the insides of the potentate as a sort of huge stomach, belongs also to another tradition, one that will be examined in chapters IX and X in terms of extreme haptics: the tradition of the body as cut up and flayed. In sixteenth-century France the image of French territory as the body of a woman ripped open was used by the Protestant writer Agrippa d'Aubigné as effective political propaganda during the religious wars.[15] A non-Western culture, the Aztec, foregrounded the image of the monarch as a heart torn out and bleeding in order to nourish the perishing world; this was the image of Quetzalcoatl. This same culture made use of a flayed body as the sign of the deity; this was the image of Xipe-Totec, who was a god of the spring revolution, of crop and flower renewal (which was the original meaning of *revolution*). And this same idea of the flayed body of the god pervaded the Mexican Revolution during the early years of this century. The heroes in the murals of Orozco, Rivera, Frida Kahlo, and, in our time, Arnold Belkin are often painted as *écorchés*, flayed alive. A section of chapter IX is devoted to this Mexican tradition.

As for the homunculus as read by the French revolutionaries, by the *sans culotte*, it will be treated in chapter VIII. The new imagery developed in the prints and broadsheets of the French *imprimeurs* after 1789 foregrounded still another organ of the human body: the scatological apparatus and its excremental functions. It is a grotesque figure, certainly more grotesque and disgusting than the Hobbesian Leviathan. Still, no picture of the grandiose and terrible period between 1789 and 1799 can be complete without it. It was during those years that a terrible kind of beauty—scurrilous and even revolting—was born. Nothing remotely similar to it has been produced since then.

Closer to us in time, the Hungarian social psychologist Imre Herrman put forward, during the 1950s, a "skin" theory or model of society—more specifically, of the borders between societies.[16] Herrman began with a reflection on the role the mother's skin plays for the child, observing that the infant adheres to its mother as though glued to her skin, so that in a first stage of development the child has to substitute its own skin (its sucked thumb) for the mother's. From this observation Herrman extrapolated in a social direction. Societies, he said, also have "skins," and there is "a skin that separates states from one another." Societies "secrete" equivalents for human skin: the borders and marginal zones, the no-man's lands, which separate them from neighboring states. "It is in these 'epidermic' regions that the first approaches toward the Foreigner, the absolute Other, take place," Herrman wrote. That, for Herrman, is the simplest manifestation of a sort of "epidermic service" that functions not on the individual level but on the societal level. Herrman seems to be especially interested in cataloging the deviant forms of this epidermic function. Thus, just as an individual, in the case of a grave neurosis or psychosis, may alienate from himself the "frontier" parts of his body, such as hair, nails, or even skin, a society alienates its borders from its center or creates new internal "skins" to marginalize zones that have been defined as irritating or dangerous.[17] This "skin" vision, according to Herrman, explains some of the metaphors used by the Nazis during the extermination of the Jews, expressions such as Himmler's "soon we shall be rid of all lice'';[18] lice are creatures which, indeed, adhere to the skin and live at the epidermic level.

After this homunculus theory has been further expounded and all the body maps, models, and metaphors have been presented, the relation of the homunculus to the optic–haptic dichotomy—that is, to theories of reading text and picture based on this dichotomy—must then be delineated in more precise terms. Attempts at reading the homunculus correspond to a haptic scanning. Only thereafter comes the textual or graphic production proper to the medium chosen by writer or painter. From this it seems obvious that there are levels of hapticity in the works that are finally produced. The flayed body and the picture or text that corresponds to it are an extreme degree of such hapticity.

VII

BODIES, MAPS, TEXTS

All the great narratives of world literature contain maps, maps that we can read. The Bible has maps of the perigrinations of Joseph, the wanderings of the Israelites in the wilderness, the Israelite invasion of the land of Canaan, and many more. The wanderings of Ulysses similarly can be traced across the Mediterranean. Maps envelop the great literary frescoes, such as the *Divine Comedy* of Dante, and the great medieval and Renaissance love poems, such as the *Romance of the Rose* and the *Faerie Queene*. Captain Ahab's search for the white whale can be transferred to marine maps, and an extraordinary scanning of a Paris street map is made by Madame Bovary as she tries to overcome her loneliness and emptiness of heart:

> She bought a map of Paris, and with her fingertips she went for walks. She followed the boulevards, stopping at every corner, between the lines indicating the streets, in front of the white squares that were the houses. Then closing her tired eyes, she would have a shadowy vision of gas lamps flickering in the wind and carriage steps clattering open in front of theaters.[1]

All these great works contain maps representing a symbolic landscape, a symbolic cartography. Yet these maps remain implicit. The first maps that were introduced explicitly into a text, appearing in extenso under their visual aspect rather than their textual one, were probably those that corresponded to allegorical narratives, such as the *carte du tendre*, the "map of tender love," which appeared around 1660 as an illustration in Mademoiselle de Scudéry's *Clélie*.[2] Another such map decorated Bunyan's *Pilgrim's Progress*.[3]

The aim of this chapter is not, however, to study maps that were used as actual illustrations for works of fiction but to examine a long metamorphosis: the process by which the human body became first a map, then a text. We shall also study the process by which texts came to be read as maps. Our final objective is to look at the metamorphosis that took place in the twentieth century by virtue of which the narrative content of a whole novel took on the shape of a gigantic human figure submerged in the text.

Many modern depictions of the body—chiefly of the female body—are anthropomorphic maps or anthropomorphic landscapes. Thus in one of Louis Aragon's love poems a woman says to her lover, "Invade me like an army / Take my plains and my hills."[4] The process of reading a poem or novel is frequently described in terms of a journey or voyage that is accomplished on a textual body seen as an actual human body. "Traveling" through *Finnegans Wake* is described as a sort of journey by a Lilliputian reader on the body of the giant Finnegan, and reading the "Anna Livia Plurabelle" chapter is like going down the Liffey, the textual river of life.

This metamorphosis was not confined to the textual level. In painting, too, bodies are turned into maps—or maps into bodies. Max Ernst's *Le jardin de la France* shows the Loire flowing around the lower part of a woman's body (fig. VII.1), and André Masson, another surrealist painter, created a series of anthropomorphic landscapes in which hills and grottoes are the breasts and genitals of a gigantic woman.[5] This idea also seems to be present in the work of contemporary painters. Alechinsky has even painted many of his productions on actual road maps of France and Europe.[6]

The Body as Map and as Text

The transformation of text into anthropomorphic map began in remote times with the metamorphosis of the cosmic map into a cosmic human body. Thus the anthropomorphization of maps preceded the cartographization of texts.

In ancient Egyptian cosmography, the vault of the sky was formed by the

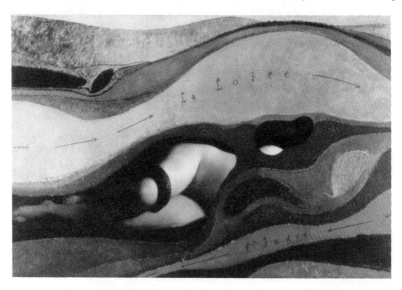

VII.1 *Le jardin de la France* by Max Ernst.
By permission of the National Museum of Modern Art/Georges Pompidou Center, Paris. Copyright by S.P.A.D.E.M. 1989.

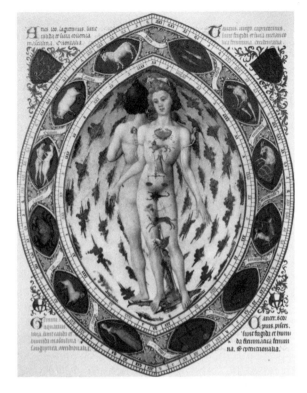

VII.2 Zodiac man.
Author's photograph.

female body of Nut, which curved like a human arch over the erect male body of Geb, the earth, and was fecundated by him. In ancient Greece, the Pythagoreans regarded the celestial bodies as so many man-shaped beings. And the Babylonians are said to have invented zodiac man, the man-shaped giant over whose body the zodiac signs were inscribed (fig. VII.2).

Jewish legends speak of a cosmic Adam, in Hebrew Adam Kadmon, "original Adam."[7] This gigantic human shape, which contained in itself all the human souls in the universe, was perhaps derived from zodiac man. It was like a map of the cosmos made up of all the individual maps, the human bodies.

In Hindu Tantrism, similarly, the universe looks like a human body and is regulated by the same laws of union and separation that regulate the sexes and their procreation. In the words of Octavio Paz, "Celestial space is not only a cosmic theater but is an extension of the human body and is in a permanent state of vibration, like a human skin."[8]

A second stage in this anthropomorphization of the map began in the Middle Ages, when the body of Christ was projected over the world map.

Thus the Erbstorff map, originally painted on the walls of the Erbstorff church during the thirteenth century and destroyed, unfortunately, during the Second World War, represented the earth-globe from which emerged the head, feet, and hands of Christ.[9] And a capital in the Spanish town of Lérida shows Christ inscribed within a circle representing the earth-globe.[10]

This projection of the body of Christ over the earth took a more sophisticated form in the work of Opicinus de Canistris during the fourteenth century, almost a century before Columbus's voyage to the New World. Opicinus made more explicit what Christian artists had begun. Their subject was not cosmic man, the starry giant who strode across the cosmos, but Christ as a flat map, a flat projection over the earth-globe. As an authoritative dictionary of symbols puts it, "The illustrations of medieval works frequently contain a Giant Christ whose body represents a scheme of the world order."[11]

The maps drafted by Opicinus do not, however, confine themselves to projections of the body of Christ. Other bodies also extend their limbs and human outlines over his cartography, as in "The Mediterranean as a Sea of Sin" (fig. VII.3), a detail from a more comprehensive map entitled "The Hierarchy of Spiritual Authority." The detail shows the outlines of Europe (on the right, or north) and Africa as a conversing man and woman, respectively. White-robed Woman, whose head is formed by the map of modern Morocco, whispers sinfully into the ear of Man, or even seems to be attempting to push her nose, the Cape of Tangier, obscenely into his ear. The man's head is Spain, his legs the Italian peninsula and the Dalmatian coast. This male figure may be an allusion to the Holy Roman Empire, since Opicinus was then living as a cleric at the court of the Avignon pope and probably considered the German emperor to be the archenemy of Avignon and of France in general.

However that may be, Opicinus's map includes Latin inscriptions that make the anthropomorphic character of his bizarre cartography even more explicit. One inscription reveals what the woman is whispering into the man's ear: *Venite commiscemini nobiscu* (Come let us copulate together). Other inscriptions reveal that Opicinus saw the map as a veritable theater of universal copulation: *femina caro (carne, corpore) corruptus, vir animus (animo) bestialis*, and so on. Thus for Opicinus earth cartography is tantamount to exposing the fornicating world. Venice, the birthplace of the cartographer, is described as a vulva open to all in a lecherous sea of sperm. It is not a question here of some Tantric eternal metamorphosis of the world through divine fornication but of a cartographer's attempt to represent the world as a netherland that embodies—incorporates—corruption and sexual sin.

Must one then see in these obsessions of Opicinus the symptoms of a personal neurosis of the artist? That was the interpretation given by the psychoanalyst Ernst Kris in a chapter entitled "A Psychotic Artist of the Middle Ages."[12] But the artist's biographer, Richard Salomon, found nothing

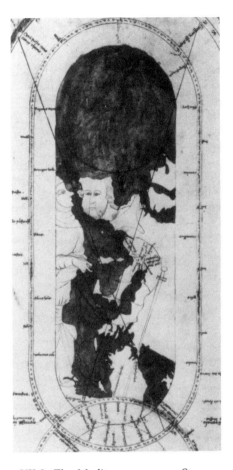

VII.3 The Mediterranean as a Sea
of Sin. An anthropomorphic map by
Opicinus de Canistris.
Photo Vatican Library; by permission.

psychopathological in his cartographic procedure.[13] Opicinus belonged to a
theological tradition that saw the earth as an underworld corresponding to
the "shameful" parts of the human anatomy. Before him, Dante, in the
Divine Comedy, used an implicit cosmography that was also anthropomorphic; his *inferno* is actually the body of Satan, a body made in the image of
man, and the hole through which Dante and Vergil issue forth from hell
onto the surface of the earth is surely Satan's penis. The implicit references
in the cartography of both the great poet and Opicinus de Canistris are but
two versions of the "erotic map of the Body-God" which Michel de Certeau
also discovered in the paintings of Bosch.[14]

A century and a half after Opicinus, the theme of Europe as anthropomorphic map became practically a genre in cartography. This was after the discovery of the New World, when map-making had reached a new peak. "Europe as Man" was seen again as a vision of the Holy Roman emperor whose crowned head was Spain, holding the earth-globe in his hand (fig. VII.4). This picture, drafted by Johannes Bucius in 1537, was one of the best known in the sixteenth century, at least among people who read books. It was reproduced more than ten times in the various editions of Münster's *Cosmography* between 1544 and 1600. It also appeared in the *Itinerarium Sacrae Scripturae* by Heinrich Bünting around 1580.

On the textual level, it is certainly the work of John Donne that corresponds most closely to this new sort of phantasmagoric cartography.

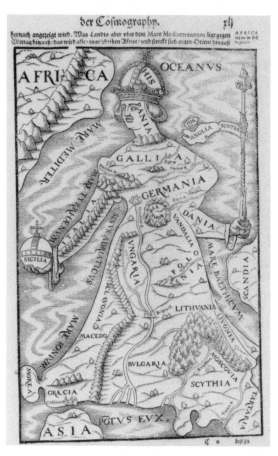

VII.4 The Holy Roman Empire as a Robed Man.
From S. Münster's *Cosmography*.
Collection of the Haifa University Library. Photo Emmanuel Gandelman.

Donne's famous sermon on the solidarity of mankind—"No man is an island, entire of it selfe"—reflects this humanized cartography. Most of Donne's so-called metaphysical poetry is also pervaded by images of maps and map-making. In his "Hymne to God" Donne describes himself as a flat map:

> Whilst my Physicians by their love are growne
> Cosmographers, and I their Mapp, who lie
> Flat on his bed. . . .
> I joy in these straits, I see my West;
> For, though their currants yield returne to none,
> What shall my West hurt me? As West and East
> In all flatt Mapps (and I am one) are one,
> So death doth touch the Resurrection.[15]

In other poems, lovers are seen as the two hemispheres of the same earth-globe:

> My face in thine eye, thine in mine appears,
> And true plaine hearts doe in the faces rest.
> Where can finde two better hemispheres
> Without sharpe North, without declining West.[16]

In "To his Mistris going to Bed" he exclaimed: "O my America: my new-found-land!"[17]

Along with the anthropomorphic tradition in map-making, another genre came to the fore on the pictorial scene during the sixteenth century: the mannerist landscape-head. Often described as Arcimboldian, these pictures (most of which, indeed, seem to be by the hand of Arcimboldo or his pupils) show gigantic faces more or less concealed in the landscape. Arcimboldo's *Landscape-Head* portrays an anthropomorphic peninsula or island bearing the features of a bearded man; the underlip is a house, the eye is the entrance to a cave, the ear is the embarcadero of a small harbor (fig. VII.5). Here, it might be said, man *is* an island!

A number of such landscapes show man not as an island but as a hill or mountain. In one of them, sometimes attributed to Joos de Momper, the seventeenth-century Dutch painter, a huge rock supporting a church and surrounded by mountain streams seems to be the face of an old man with white hair and mustache.[18]

John Donne doubtlessly was inspired by this new genre as well as by the anthropomorphic maps. In his "Loves Progress" we see a landscape à la Arcimboldo:

> The hair is a Forest of Ambushes
> The Nose (like to the first Meridian) runs
> Not 'twixt East and West but 'twixt two suns;

VII.5 *Landscape-Head* by Giuseppe Arcimboldo.
Private collection, New York; by permission. Author's photograph.

It leaves a Cheek, a rosie Hemisphere
On either side, and then directs us where
Upon the islands fortunate we fall.[19]

In French literature, a century earlier, it would not have been difficult to
find such landscapes in the work of the *grands rhétoriqueurs*. A well-known
example can be found in Rabelais's *Pantagruel* when a pilgrim who has been
swallowed by mistake by this giant king (a precursor of Hobbes's Leviathan)
finds a veritable universe—or at least an *imago mundi*—"in the mouth of
Pantagruel."[20] This conceit was, perhaps, an extrapolation from the "hell
mouth" or "mouth of heaven" so common on the fifteenth-century stage
and so often depicted in late medieval illustration. Nevertheless, it fell to
Rabelais and Arcimboldo to give a new twist to this pictorial tradition.

Arcimboldo's creations, moreover, were probably consciously ideological;
he was certainly following the advice of his friend Comanini, who, like
himself, was at the service of the king of Bohemia, Rudolf II. For Comanini, a
painter had to reproduce the face of the king "that is hidden in all the objects
within the Kingdom." How strong this tradition still is in the modern novel
can be seen in a passage from Joseph Roth's *Radetzky Marsch* in which Emperor Franz-Joseph is described in a very Arcimboldian manner: "His skull
was bald, like a desertic mound. His sideburns were white, like wings of ice.

The furrows in his face were like a disorderly forest in which centuries nestled."[21]

The Map as Text

As noted earlier, it was probably in Mademoiselle de Scudéry's novel *Clélie* that the implicit map which underlies narratives was first made explicit, being published in extenso within the text itself. The map in *Clélie* is a love map, a set of instructions in love. The instructional value of such a map must not be underestimated, yet the map's travel guide character is also obvious. The lover who reads such a love map is, as it were, traveling on the body of his or her love. This conceit was made even more explicit in the poems of Donne, where the image of making love was sometimes equated with military conquest. Another love map, which was sold as a sort of narrative game severed from a text, was called "The Attacks of Love." Devised by the German Matthias Seutter, this map, published in 1730, had captions in both German and French, such as "Symbolic and ingenious representation projected as Siege and Bombardment; how it is necessary to prevent carefully the attacks of Love."[22]

The same tendency to represent the erotic body in the form of a landscape characterized French seventeenth-century *préciosité*. One "precious" writer, Cotin (ridiculed in Molière's comedies under the name Trissotin), wrote a love poem, "L'âme immortelle," in which he speaks of the discovery by the lover of "new stars and new lands" in the soul of his mistress. Cotin's colleague Voiture described his patron Mademoiselle de Rambouillet in terms of a coastal landscape: "When I consider her calm moments, her tempest . . . her sandbanks, her cliffs and rocks . . . I am overwhelmed."[23] Although both writers were exponents of classicism, this conceit is probably more of a mannerist or baroque variation on the theme of the landscape-head than it is a description in the sense of classical antiquity.

Two centuries later we find Baudelaire's "La chevelure," in which the lover engulfs himself in the hair of his mistress and sees himself as a navigator lost on an exotic ocean:

> Sweltering Africa and langorous Asia,
> A whole far-away world, absent, almost defunct,
> Dwells in your depths, aromatic forest!
> While other spirits glide on the wings of music,
> Mine, O my love! floats upon your perfume. . . .
> I shall bury my head enamored with rapture
> In this black ocean where the other sea is imprisoned
> And my subtle spirit caressed in the rolling
> Will find you once again, O fruitful indolence,
> Endless lulling of sweet centered leisure![24]

Baudelaire did not know the work of Opicinus de Canistris, but he was certainly aware of the existence of the genre of the human-shaped cosmographic map. His essay on Victor Hugo contains these lines: "Swedenborg had already told us [that is, before Hugo] that the sky is a gigantic man. . . ."[25] As a matter of fact, many poems in *The Flowers of Evil*, such as "The Giant Woman" and "The Cat," seem to be placed under the aegis of the "voyage in the body of the Other"—that is, of the female Other.

Baudelaire helped metamorphose the precious beauty of mannerism, the beauty of the metaphysical poetry of Donne, into a dark terrible beauty, and his imagery had an important influence over the iconography of its time. I am thinking particularly of some pictures of Munch, who lived in Paris in the 1880s. These pictures (*Lover in the Waves, Madonna, Man and Woman,* and others[26]) show a man lost in the mane of his beloved's hair. This immense mane seems to have become a dark cosmic river in which men drown. This development is one more stage, a relay, on the way to our ultimate objective: the transformation through which the text itself becomes a map and invites us readers to read it or to read in it as we travel with our eyes over the text.

The Text as Map

The general physiognomy or anatomy of *Finnegans Wake* as a giant half-buried in the Irish landscape has been commented on by several literary critics. Joseph Campbell wrote that Joyce's novel "opens like a Baedeker. It is a bulky guide which may be used to visit a vast, strangely sleepy and unstable landscape: the inside of a human being."[27] And again: "The scene is disintegrating. The outlines of hills seem to appear under the outlines of the Wake. Hurra! The form of Finnegan is that of the landscape."[28]

If one goes deeper into the book, it is possible to discover still more outlines of the giant Finnegan asleep; the figure becomes a sort of watermark on most of the novel's pages: "Yet may we not see still the brontoyichtian form outlined aslumbered, even in our own nighttime by the sedge of the troutling stream. . . . The cranic head on him, caster of his reasons, peer yuthner in yondmist. Wooth?"[29] The "Anna Livia Plurabelle" chapter describes woman—that is, an archetype with a woman's body—as a great river, introducing stream topography into the book: "Rise it, flut ye, pian piena: I'm dying off my iodine feet. . . ."[30] And Anna Livia suddenly screams: "By earth and cloudy but I badly want a brandnew bankside!"[31] She sees herself as flowing "fiffty odd Irish miles" through the Irish landscape.[32]

Gigantic human shapes are concealed beneath a sort of topographic-linguistic carapace. The reader who wishes to discern the body of Finnegan or of Anna Livia in more detail must make considerable effort. But it is precisely the sort of effort also asked of us when we read in depth the reversible landscape-heads of the sixteenth and seventeenth centuries. Like

VII.6 *The Story of a River,* a book cover
by Margaret MacDonald.
*Author's collection. Photo Emmanuel
Gandelman.*

Arcimboldo, James Joyce was a master of the permanent reversibility of
forms.

The period when *Finnegans Wake* was written actually saw a revival in
painting of the mannerist genre of the landscape-head. For example, *The
Story of a River,* a picture by Margaret MacDonald, the companion and then
the wife of Charles Rennie MacIntosh, a leader of the art nouveau movement in England at the turn of the century, depicts a woman as a river with
what looks like "iodine feet" (fig. VII.6). It seems to have been drafted many
years before Joyce started working on his "Anna Livia Plurabelle," but here
too we see the woman flowing her "fiffty odd Irish miles" in the textual
landscape.

The revival was not limited to art nouveau. The German expressionists
also saw landscapes in terms of human physiognomy. Emil Nolde's *The
Matterhorn Is Smiling* shows a mountain with a human face,[33] and *Nach der
Schlacht* (After the battle) by Alfred Kubin depicts a flight of crows swooping

down over a mountain chain whose outlines are those of a gigantic dead body.[34] Paul Klee, a refugee from the expressionist movement, sketched a *Landschaftlich-Physiognomisch* (Physiognomic landscape).[35]

In the 1930s, when Joyce was working on the final draft of *Finnegans Wake*, propaganda posters were presenting huge heads of leaders and politicians as composite Leviathans. The Soviet constructivist El Lissitzki made a photomontage representing the head of Lenin as constituted by the Russian masses.[36] Similar heads by Italian publicists showed Mussolini's head made out of shots of the Italian masses raising their hands in the Fascist salute.[37] Even in the United States a poster by George Beall depicted the head of Franklin Roosevelt as a composite made up of recognizable American types and landscapes.[38] It is hardly imaginable that Joyce was not influenced, at least indirectly, by this international visual context in which brutal giants so shamelessly presented their powerful faces to the world in terms of anthropomorphic maps of their homelands as they were preparing to rush about Europe and trample it under their iron heels.

Also at about the same time Joyce was writing *Finnegans Wake*, two other great writers, Henri Michaux and Juan Luis Borges, were preparing literary masterpieces that featured the appearance of human bodies or faces. Michaux wrote in his prose text "My Properties":

> These properties are my only properties and I have been living in them since my early childhood. . . . This is due to the fact that I have been condemned to live in these properties: I must make the most of them. . . . I prepare a jaw, a digestive apparatus and an excretory one; as soon as the outer envelope is ready, I insert the pancreas and the liver. . . . Yet teeth suddenly seem to be missing; then soon it is the turn of the jaw, then the liver, and when I reach the anus, I remain there with the anus in my hand: this is disgusting. . . .[39]

Obviously Michaux's "properties" make up his own body, his own anatomy. In another of Michaux's works, *Paix dans les brisements* (Peace within rupture), one reads: "I am a stream in the midst of the stream that carries me away." A series of hallucinated drawings that illustrates this text reproduces this stream; it also shows the fundamental split in this continuous consciousness stream.[40]

These words of Michaux repeat or prefigure similar ones by Borges: "the stream is carrying me away, yet I *am* the stream." The face of Borges emerges sporadically from the aleph in his story by that name. This magic letter contains the whole world in the form of pictures and representations of all sorts which ceaselessly succeed one another. The face of Borges superimposed over the world is like a double of this world. Conversely, the world is the double of Borges's face:

> A man sets himself the task of sketching the world. As years go by, he peoples his space with images, with provinces, with kingdoms, with mountains, bays,

ships, islands, fish, rooms, instruments, planets, horses, persons. A little before he is going to die, he discovers that this patient labyrinth of lines delineates the picture of his own face.[41]

A later development in the same direction comes in Stanley Kubrick's *2001: A Space Odyssey*. Toward the end of this film, the journey into space turns into a journey through the body or features of the voyager himself. What the spectator had taken at first to be a series of planets and space valleys turns out to be the eyeballs and the furrows in the face of the hero himself, the outlines of his face. The journey through space is revealed as a journey through Self.

This general direction of literature and cinema toward the fusion of two species of space—interior and planetary—seems to have its counterpart in modern psychoanalytic investigations. Lacan used the image of the anthropomorphic map in his seminar on "The Purloined Letter," the Edgar Allan Poe story. Lacan described the letter as "un gigantesque corps de femme" sprawling in the minister's study. The Lacanian paradox is that this huge female body is never identified as a body—is not even seen—by the observers; the map is never used as a map. In terms of our cortical homunculus, this means a *dénégation* of the very possibility of representation. For Lacan, this paradox represents the quintessence of the phenomenon of *dénégation*.

Lacan himself is closer to Opicinus de Canistris and Arcimboldo than one might think. His work is essentially a very personal description of the unconscious in terms of its topology and cartography. This psychoanalyst sees our selves as so many anthropomorphic maps, just as dreams—at least many of those recorded in Freud's *Interpretation of Dreams*—describe our selves in terms of landscape-heads or landscape-bodies. All the various models used by Lacan (the Möbius strips, the Borromean knots, and so on) reflect his essential objective of describing the topographic psyche that is implicit within us all.

VIII

THE SCATOLOGICAL HOMUNCULUS

An indelicate imagery that appeared after 1789 in the prints and broadsheets of French *imprimeurs* foregrounds a part of human anatomy that usually remains in the background: the excremental apparatus and its functions. The French revolutionaries saw the face of the king as a limp penis and the human body as a huge defecating organ, a sort of loaded gun they could train on their enemies.[1] This revolutionary homunculus is a grotesque figure, certainly more disgusting than Hobbes's Leviathan. Still, no portrait of the grandiose and terrible period between 1789 and 1799 would be complete without it.[2]

One cannot fail to be impressed by the quality and quantity of monographs devoted to the revolution's "reasonable" imagery, its "emblems of reason." Mona Ozouf's *La fête révolutionnaire*, for example, is concerned almost entirely with the allegorical, neoclassical aspect of its processions and decorations. Precious few studies are devoted to its scatology, though the scurrilous images are there for all to see.[3] Unfortunately, these images do not fit into the customary headings provided by scholars of art history such as Jean Starobinsky and Ernst Gombrich; *les emblèmes de la raison* and *les blasons de la liberté* just won't do.[4] In fact, they are so scurrilous and so numerous as to warrant a reexamination of the very idea that reason was a preeminent ideal of that upheaval.

This lack of attention may simply reflect the human tendency to avoid unsavory topics.[5] Even in our time, when most things sexual may be freely mentioned, the excremental functions are still unwelcome conversation pieces. Such offensive smut is also considered no proper object of research by many historians. Nevertheless, the excremental apparatus appears to be the most visible body organ in the verbal and graphic productions of revolutionary France. What does the omnipresence of this scatology in the imagery of the French Revolution signify? Can it yield clues to the meaning of the revolution?

The Corpus

A corpus of representative pictures will serve to illustrate my thesis. Although data are unavailable, the great number of scatological prints on

VIII.1 *Lilliput* by Vivan-Denon.
Author's collection and photograph.

the market in the teeming streets of the French capital during the years
that shook eighteenth-century Europe can be guessed at from the descriptions by Fuchs and others of the intensity of later efforts of the Restoration
police to destroy them.[6] One thing is certain: the proliferation of erotic and
scatological pictures reached its peak in the first years of the revolution,
1790 to 1792. As an almanac of the period noted, the obscene broadsheets
"are found more than anywhere else in the pocket of those who condemn
them."[7] It is probably also true that the phrase *chez tous les libraires* ("in all
bookshops"), frequently written on the pamphlets' covers or underneath
the broadsheets, reflected the true situation in a city where royalty was
still maintained nominally on the throne with all the usual outward trap-
pings of power when it had no real power anymore, including the power
of censorship and even the more elementary one of protecting its own
privacy and public image.

The Limp Penis

Some of the new scurrilous imagery on the open market represented the
king as a powerless or impotent male sex organ, including two pictures by
Vivan-Denon, a painter about whom quite a few biographical details have
been preserved in the biographical encyclopedias on artists (figs. VIII.1 and 2).
The king is not referred to by name, but the year in which these pictures

VIII.2 *The King of Kings* by Vivan-Denon.
Author's collection and photograph.

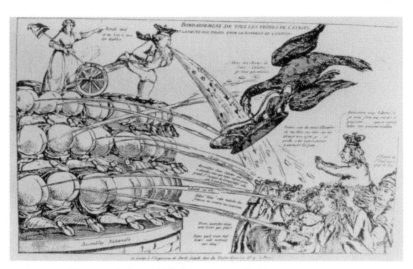

VIII.3 Bombardement de tous les trônes de l'Europe.
Author's collection and photograph.

appeared leaves no doubt about the identity of the monarch they stand for. These etchings apparently were published in the *Etrennes aux fouteurs* of 1790.[8]

One can certainly regard these two pictures as metonymic representations of Louis XVI. They are also signs of the death of the king. In other words, the actual beheading of Louis was but the finale to a series of representations in which the king had been described as already sexually dead.

Defecation

The human body—that is, the bodies of the *sans culottes* who claimed to stand for the whole of humanity—became a sort of scatological cannon bombarding the crowned heads of Europe (fig. VIII.3). This caricature bears the indication that it could be bought, if not in all bookshops, at least in the Cercle Soant, the Soant Club, in the Rue du Théâtre Français. It is an exact translation of the term *sans culottes:* the *sans culottes* who formed the rank and file of the National Assembly have doffed their *culottes,* their pants, to bombard the monarchs of Europe with their defecations. Similarly, the Republic uses the body of the king as a veritable mouthpiece for the Republican gun which projects the vomit of Louis XVI onto the heads of his fellow monarchs. This same analogy, body = cannon, is explicit in another picture, in which the king of Prussia is shown aiming his "gun" at the Republic while Louis XVI shouts to him: "I advise you to do what I have been doing for years: kissing her . . ." (fig. VIII.4).

These caricatures are not only visual entertainments or visual provocations. They also translate popular execration phrases, such as "J'emmerde le

VIII.4 "Do what I have been doing for years. . . ."
Author's collection and photograph.

roi, les nobles, le clergé." Thus a soldier of the revolutionary army defecates on the clergy and nobility sunk in a cesspool (fig. VIII.5).

Other caricatures show *sans culottes* wiping their bottoms with official declarations by king or clergy (fig. VIII.6). This particular *sans culotte* is wiping his behind with a papal brief condemning the new constitution. This brief is probably shown as it was reproduced in the royalist paper *L'Ami du Roi*, since the signature of the editor of this paper, L'Abbé Royou, is clearly shown in a corner of the printed sheet. The man, incidentally, is wearing the *culotte*, the sign of the ancien régime. He is actually shown in the process of becoming a *sans culotte*, doffing his old-fashioned breeches; a scatological act is equated with revolutionary action. Again, this picture represents the translation of such popular expressions as "Je m'en torche le cul" and "Je me le fous au cul." For the artist, then, to accomplish the revolution was to translate into visual terms the language of popular derision and popular wrath.

Quite a few prints show the birth of the enemy through the excremental apparatus. That is the case with a picture directed against Abbé Maury (fig. VIII.7). It bears the inscription:

> On April the 13th, 1790, two flying devils
> Made a wager:
> Which one would defecate the more stinking creature
> Over human nature?
> One shit Abbot M . . . y
> The other went all pale
> And dropped D'E . . . y
> And all his pals.

It is also the case with another picture more generally directed against the aristocracy and entitled "Naissance des Aristocrates" (fig. VIII.8). Such rep-

VIII.5 "My trick; this time they won't ever come back!"
Photo Bibliothèque Nationale, Paris; by permission.

resentations resemble what Freud would later call the infantile theory on birth, a subject in which Melanie Klein was to specialize.

Purging

The excremental act of purging is also frequently represented (fig. VIII.9). Actually, this word *purging* occurred frequently in speeches at the National Assembly, including a famous one by Garnier de Saintes on the 10th of Germinal of Year II: "If we are purging, it is in order to obtain the right to purge France. We shall leave no heterogeneous body in the Republic."[9] But the extreme form of purgation, let us not forget, was achieved later, by the infamous invention of Dr. Guillotin.

Spanking

Many pictures represent revolutionary victory in the form of a Republican spanking his adversary or enemy. Such is the case in a picture in which General Jourdan is shown triumphing over Cobourg (fig. VIII.10). Of special significance for this study is the fact that Cobourg's behind shows the armories of Austria, the double-headed eagle, and is, in some way, the face of

VIII.6 The Papal Brief.
*By permission of the Bibliothèque
Nationale, Paris.*

Austria. The unveiling of Cobourg's bottom thus is tantamount to showing the face of the king.

Whose Progeny?

The images found in our corpus were not the sole invention of *sans culottes* propaganda. An iconographic filiation for the pictorial scatology of the revolutionaries stretches across two centuries.

There is, most noticeably, what one might call a Rabelaisian continuity. The popularity of Rabelais in *sans culottes* France was tremendous. The revolutionaries saw him as one of their forefathers, as Bakhtin noted: "He was even made out to be a prophet of the revolution. His hometown of Chinon was renamed Chinon-Rabelais." Bakhtin further stated that the most important document related to this subject was Guiguené's book published in 1791, "Of the influence of Rabelais on the revolution of our time and on the decree concerning the clergy."[10] I would add that Guiguené also praises Rabelais for presenting the body of the king as a grotesque and boundless stomach bent on devouring the food of the people.

The sixteenth century is also present as cited tradition in another picture of the period, in which a *sans culotte* draftsman named Langlois saw royalist Europe as an assembly of defecating monarchs (fig. VIII.11). The inspiration, if not Rabelaisian, is definitely of sixteenth-century origin, for the picture is entitled "Vanitas" and this genre, which was created at the beginning of the

VIII.7 Two Devils in a Furor.
Photo Bibliothèque Nationale, Paris;
by permission.

baroque period, became definitely canonical in the second half of the sixteenth century.[11]

The biographies of specific draftsmen yield additional clues as to filiation.
Vivan-Denon, the author of two of the obscene etchings already presented,
figures VIII.1 and 2, seems to have been a defrocked abbot. As such, he must
certainly have been familiar with the antichurch propaganda of previous
centuries.[12] Like many *défroqués,* Vivan-Denon transformed his allegiance to
pope and church into a ferocious hatred, which was nourished by the history
of the events of the first revolution against the pope, the Reformation. Other
revolutionary artists may have had Hugeunot backgrounds and may therefore have been acquainted with the antipapist propaganda of the Reformation, upon which they may have drawn for their own creations.[13]

Certainly the filiation of such pictures as the one representing the spanking of Cobourg, figure VIII.10, may date back to the time of the Reformation,
for we have a picture from that time which is almost identical (fig. VIII.12).
These is no doubt that in spanking their opponents the revolutionaries

VIII.8. Birth of the Aristocrats.
Photo Bibliothèque Nationale, Paris; by permission.

appropriated the gesture of the father. The enemies were more than just enemies; they were rioting children who had to be ruled. This type of image is, in a way, very close to the upside-down world of sixteenth-century iconography, in which children were shown spanking their fathers.[14]

It is well known that the iconography of the topsy-turvy world constitutes a large corpus of iconographical material, and it is not absent from the iconography of the French Revolution. As early as 1789, popular engravings presented the upheaval in the form of a peasantlike figure standing for the third estate and perched on the back of a nobleman who hangs onto the cassock of a priest. The peasant is shouting, "J'savions bien qu'j'aurions not' tour" ("I knew I would have my turn"—at being the rider).[15] This caricature corresponds almost exactly to sixteenth-century broadsheets showing a servant taking his master to prison, or a peasant being on a horse while, beside him, the kings goes on foot.[16]

In the prerevolutionary eighteenth century there also had been many pictures of erotic *fessées* mutually given and received by nuns and monks in the convents of France. They were circulated sub rosa by the libertines. And that

VIII.9 "I told you, friend, they would make
us give back everything!"
*Photo Bibliothèque Nationale, Paris;
by permission.*

raises the question of the relation between libertinism and revolutionary
scatology.

The libertine tradition actually served as a bridge between sixteenth-
century imagery and revolutionary scatology.[17] A number of anonymous
sans culottes artists had undoubtedly followed this tradition during the ancien régime. In the post-Reformation world from the seventeenth century
onward, the main way artists and writers had to express their atheism or
anticlericalism was to indulge in sex and its representation. Fornication or
the description of fornication was tantamount to an atheist profession of
faith. The seventeenth-century character of Don Juan, for example, was libertine; indeed, it may be claimed that Don Juan was from the outset a sort of
anthropomorphization of the erect penis—Priapus as the antithesis of the
cross.

There is little doubt that Vivan-Denon belonged to the libertine current
before the revolution.[18] Another painter—a greater one than Vivan-
Denon—had also been connected with libertinism: Jacques Louis David. David did not hesitate to turn to obscenity in some of his cartoons in defense of
the Republic. Both men were among those who politicized the representation of the male sexual organs.

The scurrilous imagery of the Reformation probably found its source in
the scatology of its greatest leader, Martin Luther. When Luther shouted at
the devil to "note this down: I have shit in the pants and you may wear
them around your neck and wipe your mouth with it!" he was convinced
that he had flung the ultimate insult, the ultimate projectile. According to
Luther's biographer, the psychoanalyst Erik Erikson, the anal insult was

VIII.10 A Republican Spanking.
Photo Bibliothèque Nationale, Paris; by permission.

indeed what Luther thought the devil feared most. Luther believed that "the devil expressed his scorn by exposing his rear parts: man can beat him to it by employing anal weapons and by telling him where his kiss is welcome."[19] That is exactly what the *sans culottes* are saying in their scurrilous images, especially in figure VIII.4, which shows the king of France kissing Liberty's behind.[20]

The explanation given by Erikson for this kind of behavior in Luther is not convincing: "To confront the devil in his position means to offer him the

VIII.11 Revolutionary Vanitas.
Author's collection and photograph.

VIII.12 Nun Spanking a Monk.
Reformation period.
Author's collection and photograph.

other set of cheeks." I would suggest that it is a whole human physiognomy of a specific kind that was offered to the gaze of the "aristocratic devils" by the *sans culottes*.

At any rate, we see that revolutionary images not only showed the enemy's behind, caught with his pants down, but also, as a metaphor, exposed the revolutionaries' own behind to the enemy. In doing so, the revolutionaries perhaps aimed to immobilize this enemy, somewhat as it was done in classical myths. But instead of showing their foes the awful head of Medusa, the *sans culottes* drew a "face" that these foes were at once unable and yet able to recognize. We will see what this face was at the conclusion of this chapter.

There is also in the pictures in our corpus, as in the Lutheran pamphlets at the time of the Reformation, an inversion between uterus and intestine, a transfer of the functions of parturition to the digestive functions. This inversion is all the more striking in a cartoon by David, showing the king of England as a doublefaced devil, the second face being in the place of his behind (fig. VIII.13).

The birth of the enemy through the rectum was a favorite insult of Luther's.[21] Was it not Luther who advised the young Cranach concerning the proper manner in which to reproduce the birth of the pope and his prelates (fig. VIII.14)? Many Protestant artists followed suit. A well-known picture by an anonymous artist entitled *Die Erschaffung der Mönche* shows a brood of monks being born from a devil in a similar manner.[22] Thus this conceit, like much of the rest of the French revolutionary scatology, is in the direct line of the anal insult as it was practiced in the Reformation.

VIII.13 *The English Government* by Jacques Louis David.
Photo Bibliothèque Nationale, Paris; by permission.

The Question of Meaning

We have now reached the end of our scatological corpus. What remains to be dealt with is the question of meaning. Several possibilities of approaching this meaning have already emerged. First is the question of the philosophical basis of scatology. The second important query concerns the place of scatology within the revolutionary feast—or, perhaps better, antifeast. The third question to be dealt with is that of the image as a translation of popular scatological language into visuality and the function of such a translation. And finally we will examine what may be a deeper signification of the scatological, perhaps with reference to depth psychology; in particular, what does the *ostentio* of the human excremental apparatus really mean?

Philosophy

The philosophical support for the type of revolutionary imagery we have been looking at doubtlessly was the materialism of the Lumières, such figures as the Baron d'Holbach and La Mettrie. This materialism is graphically

VIII.14 *Birth of the Pope and His Monks*
by Cranach.
Author's photograph.

presented in La Mettrie's book *L'homme machine,* in which man is seen as a
sui generis organism that lives and dies just as a machine does.[23]

In many ways, the work of La Mettrie was more revolutionary than Marat's *De l'homme,* a work in which the future editor of *L'Ami du Peuple*
showed that he adhered fundamentally to the "double substance" theory of
Descartes.[24] Marat's language is never scatological; he never stoops to using
expressions of the people, whom he ostensibly loved so much. For the popu-
list revolutionaries, the Hébertistes, however, to proclaim oneself a defecating machine meant to proclaim the supremacy of matter and of materialism;
it meant to foreground the inescapable presence of the body in the midst of
the idealistic discourse of their enemies at the National Assembly. To proclaim oneself a defecating machine was to project the base image of the body
over against the dazzling rhetoric of the idealistic Jacobins, with their abstract concept of some Supreme Being.

This overt presentation of man as a shitting and fucking machine seems to
have been widespread in the Paris of the first years of the revolution. In the
same publication that printed the etchings of Vivan-Denon, the *Etrennes aux
fouteurs* (which translates as "A present for the fuckers"), one finds these

verses, directed against the queen and alluding to the supposed lasciviousness of the royal spouse:

> Depuis qu'une Autrichienne en rut
> A tout venant montre le cul
> Depuis qu'on placa l'optimisme
> Dans l'ovale humide et charnu
> Qui produit notre mécanisme. . . .[25]

There is no doubt that the word *mécanisme* is of great significance here. It points to the "homme machine" elaborated upon by La Mettrie. In this way the anonymous rhymester aimed to present himself as an heir to the *philosophes.*

Indeed, it could be claimed that a struggle between two philosophical currents simmered throughout the French Revolution. One of them put to the fore the Cartesian idea of a two-substance duality in man and was represented by Marat and by Robespierre, among others. The other current was rooted in the thought of the materialist philosophers of the preceding generation. Ironically, it was the organicists who actually amputated the organic royal body.

Neither Marat nor Robespierre saw man—or the state which rules man—in any fundamentally different way from that which prevailed in prerevolutionary days. They upheld the idea of government as a well-tempered, harmonious body, with a "head," the state, resting smoothly on the limbs and organs that were the citizens, just as the idea of the king as head and his subjects as limbs had been upheld in the past.

There was, however, something radically new in the presentation of the state—be it king, national assembly, or army—as a defecatory organ in the left-wing and the scatological press. But we are still far from knowing exactly what this emphasis on the excremental functions of the political homunculus really means.

The Antifête

A ludic function also comes to the fore in this bandying about of excrements. Scatology was an outburst of revolutionary rejoicing, but it had more to do with *la vrai fête révolutionnaire* than with the official celebration.

It is no secret that the French revolutionaries lacked humor. One might even speak of a constitutional humorlessness. One does not joke, after all, about the new society one has helped to create, whose midwife one has been, as it were. And so *la fête révolutionnaire* did not laugh very much. Mona Ozouf devoted only one page to a description of "l'autre fête," that is, the feast with a truly carnivalesque character. The officially organized feast was serious, dealt exclusively in the glorification of the Republic, and claimed to reproduce the earnestness of the virtuous Roman Republic it saw as its ancestor. This official feast was essentially allegorical, even neoclassical, in character. It was a sort of triumph of neoclassicism and allegory per se.

The scatological element may be seen as a return of a carnival spirit with its glorification of the upside down, which is almost completely absent from allegorical rejoicing. In this sense, the scatological imagery is an upside-down structure inside an upside-down structure. This is pure dialectics: the ancien régime was an upside-down world which has now been set right, but neoclassical allegory, which represents this setting right, must now in turn be upturned to make room for the laughter of the people. Thus the return of the carnival comes about through the agency of the scatological, not through the activity of the organizers of the official celebration.

Translation

But scatology is more than an outlet for humor as against neoclassical seriousness. It is also a showcase for language at its basest: a projection of the language of the people into the visual field. I have already noted the close relationship between the scatological imagery and the language of the populace. The French of the people was fraught—as it still is today—with such expressions as "Tu me fais chier" and "Tu m'emmerdes." An old popular song contains the lines "J'emmerde les gendarmes / Et la maréchaussée."

What the people saw in the profusion of these scatological images was its own language in visual form. Language, being projected into the medium of the visual, the base language of the people, was accessible to everybody. There was no need to be literate to know what was being said about power and the exponents of power. Thus scatology became an ideogram of the language of the *sans culottes*. And this language was also a setting upside down of heroic "neoclassical" rhetoric.

The depiction of the enemy as a "behind-faced" person, for example, is tantamount to asserting that he is an upside-down man, just as his world is an upside-down world. In the jokes of the *sans culottes* the nobles were sometimes designated as *ci-derrières* ("those from behind") rather than the usual *ci-devants* ("those from before"). There are some well-known but untranslatable verses concerning "Monsieur le Ci-Devant Derrière," Monsieur de la Villette, known for his lascivious appetites:

> Quand Villette apprenait à lire
> Jamais un R il ne put dire
> Son précepteur fut convaincu
> Qu'il resterait toujours au Q.[26]

And the *Rocambole des Journaux*, a sort of entertainment guide of the period, announced the opening of a play called *Les sans-devant derrière, opéra à machine*.

Through the foregrounding of his defecating functions, the *ci-devant* be-comes a "machine" that functions *à l'envers*, in reverse. He is essentially a producer of waste, of garbage, the inverse of a real *producteur*, a worker. That is also the meaning of our extremely obscene "Vanitas," figure VIII.11, probably published in the mid-nineties. All this scatology is a reminder that the *ci-devant* world was also an upside-down world in which topsy-turvy relations were the rule. But it can be further construed as a projection of the language of the people into the visual field, as an ideogram signifying the power of the people's language.

In many ways, the printed images circulated or sold on the streets must have played the role that is played today by the visual media and especially television. Petit bourgois ideology keeps complaining that today's pop cul-ture is a culture for the illiterate. The same probably was said about the broadsheet pictures on Paris streets at the time of the revolution.

The language of the pictures is instantaneously grasped and gives the people a feeling of immediacy. That is never the case with the written lan-guage of the papers, even when this language is produced in oral form by public reading. The decipherability and success of the sometimes very com-plex images I have presented were due in large extent to a phenomenon of recognition: the populace recognized in them its own language, its own ex-pressions, but in another form, a medium that made the words more po-tent—for visibility, in those days, *was* potency, as it is in our day.

A Deeper Significance

The analogy face = behind has already been noted. In figure VIII.10, for example, Cobourg or Austria is a behind spanked by Jourdan. The caricature by David, figure VIII.13, is even more explicit. Its "Explication" makes clear that the king of England's behind is also his face, or one of his faces. What sense is there in all of this? What sense are we to make of this *ostentio*, this pointing to the behind as face?

The historian who deals with such material today cannot help seeing it through the eyes of other historians of a special type, who have attempted to make sense of similar material. These special historians are the psycho-pathologists such as Krafft-Ebbing, the anthropologists such as Bourke, and the psychoanalysts such as Freud and Erikson.[27]

It is Freud, I believe, who gives us the key to the enigma in a short essay—actually a case study—called "A Mythological Parallel to a Visual Obses-sion."[28] A young man, who Freud reported was hounded by the vision of his father's face as a "behind," revealed that he also thought of his father as the "patriarch." *Arch* in German slang means "asshole." His father was, there-fore, the *Vater-Arch*. Similarly, the French revolutionaries, I suspect, were saying that the archfather of the people, the king, was in reality the father-asshole. They of course did not think in German, but the idea of the king-father as behind, as asshole, was a "visual obsession" in their imagery. It was their desire to overturn the king and nobles, to set them upside down—the meaning of *revolution* at its most concrete—that led them to this type of representation.

Freud also tells us something about the nature of the symbolic efficacy (to use Lévi-Strauss's term) of the *ostentio*, the exposing of one's hind parts to the enemy.[29] The idea is to show him what the father's face really looks like. Revolutionary images show, as it were, their hind parts to the world in order to stun it, to fascinate it, and finally to immobilize it.[30] The suggested analogy is to the face of Medusa, which Freud interpreted as actually a presentation of the mother's sexual organs.

Bataille insisted upon it: man cannot look sex, the genitalia, "in the eye."[31] Similarly, man, or at least counterrevolutionary man, cannot look his father in the eye, cannot bear to glance at the uncanny face that is at once so strange and so familiar.

But these pictures also have another purpose. The scatology in the imagery of the revolution can be seen as a justification of revolutionary violence. If scatological imagery corresponds to the infantile theories of birth through the excremental apparatus, if the enemy is shown as being born through the sphincter, it is only in order to expose him as a *kakon*. Psychoanalysis has shown, almost from the very beginning, that the phantasm of the enemy as *kakon* is at the root of the aggressive and sadistic tendencies of the ideology of violence, the ideology that demands the extermination of the Other. In the ultimate analysis, it may be said that it was for the purgation of such human excrement that the guillotine was invented.

Making sense of the scatological imagery of the French Revolution has necessarily meant reading the "revolutionary" body image behind the caricature, reading the homunculus that functioned as an algorithm for the *sans culotte* draftsman. We have seen in preceding chapters that texts can be read as bodies, sometimes as gesture, sometimes as map. Now we see that pictures belonging to the sphere of political propaganda can be read as the surface appearances of an internalized homunculus that foregrounds now the head, now the eyes, now the hands—and now the excremental organs—of the implicit human body it contains.

IX

HAPTICS IN EXTREMIS

We saw in the first chapter that looking at a picture haptically means focus-ing on the picture's surface as if to touch it or penetrate it. By this definition there is one type of intensified vision that deserves to be called haptics in extremis, an excess of hapticism: the X-ray vision invented by Röntgen at the end of the nineteenth century. This vision truly penetrates the human anat-omy and achieves a sort of visual dissection of the body.

As X rays became common in the medical world, the term was put to use as a metaphor by art critics. In the first decade of this century, for instance, Oskar Kokoschka, the expressionist painter, was said to paint as though through the medium of X rays.[1] A self-portrait exhibited at the Kunstschau in Vienna in 1909 was described by one of Kokoschka's first biographers as "the most extraordinary object of the whole exhibition. . . . It was a sort of caricatural skull which only vaguely resembled its model, brutally marked with little blue veins at the placing of the cheeks, the tongue pointed be-tween grimacing lips." This biographer, leaving no doubt about the source of the painter's inspiration, added: "This horrible spectre was a sort of hybrid between an Oceanic mask and an anatomical specimen."[2] This self-portrait has disappeared, and today we can see the work only in a photographic reproduction.[3] It confirms the biographer's assertion that Kokoschka drew his inspiration from an anatomical model, a sort of flayed body.

The motif of the flayed body first appeared in Kokoschka's work in 1908 in four illustrations for a play Kokoschka wrote, *Mörder, Hoffnung der Frauen* (Murderer, hope of women). The illustrations show Man and Woman en-gaged in mutually flaying each other's body (fig. IX.1). This seemingly cruel penetration beneath the epidermis was Kokoschka's metaphor for love.

Even more penetrating is the poster Kokoschka made to advertise the first night of his play (fig. IX.2). In books devoted to the painter, this poster is usually labeled "Pietà," although nothing about it warrants such a name. What in fact is seen in this picture is not a woman holding her dead son in her arms but a livid creature, a man, who seems to have undergone a flaying operation—the veins and nerves in his face are no longer covered by skin. The man's features remind one of the young Kokoschka in the *Portrait of the Painter Pointing at Himself* (1913), for example, or the various self-portraits in

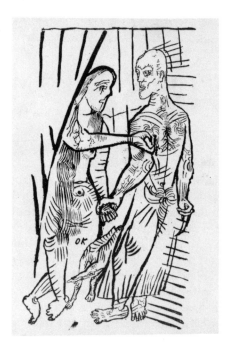

IX.1 Illustration from *Mörder, Hoffnung
der Frauen* by Kokoschka.
Author's collection and photograph.

the *Bachkantate* (1914).[4] This figure holds in his clawlike hands what looks
like the corpse of another human being but in reality is his own bleeding
skin. The position of the hands suggests that he has torn his own skin off,
rather as one removes an old garment that fits too tightly. What we have
here, in perhaps the first series of art works that can truly be called expressionist, is a depiction of self-flaying.

Mannerism, Marsyas, and Michelangelo

Where did this theme come from? Were there iconographical precedents
for Kokoschka's pictures? To my mind, it can safely be said that the motif
was a revival of the mannerist theme of self-flaying. Of course, expressionism has often been described as a revival of sixteenth-century mannerism.[5]
Yet, surprisingly, it has never been examined from the point of view of the
motifs it inherited or borrowed from mannerist iconography.

The flayed man motif in mannerism was the outcome of a dialectical

IX.2 Poster for *Mörder, Hoffnung der Frauen*
by Kokoschka.
Author's photograph.

inversion. It emerged at a moment when the product of the systematic scientific exploration of the body—the reproduction through sketches and drawings of subcutaneous anatomy and internal organs—modulated into an artistic genre. Art appeared at the very moment when the shapes and figures that are revealed when the body is disjointed and dissected ceased to be strictly scientific and became "aesthetic." Sixteenth-century man, who had lived through the terrible sacking of Rome in 1527 and the no less horrible religious wars, apparently found pleasure in seeing his interior mechanism laid bare. Certainly some of the great draftsmen from the sixteenth century to the end of the eighteenth century taxed their macabre imaginations to make their figures of the flayed human body turn into creatures of fantastic art rather than dry representations belonging strictly to medical or anatomical science.

Thus the *écorchés* in Vesalius's *De humanis corpore fabrica*, drawn by Johannis Von Kalkar—one of the first works that can be described as mannerist—and subsequently those by Charles Estienne in *De dissectione partium corporis humani* assume affectedly elaborate poses and sometimes even seem

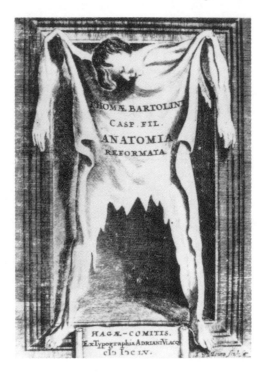

IX.3 Frontispiece to Bartolini's *Anatomia
reformata*; probably a self-portrait of Bartolini.
Author's collection.

to make erotic or obscene gestures. They are products of the taste for *terribilità* so characteristic of mannerism.[6]

By the beginning of the seventeenth century the flayed body had become a decorative motif. The frontispiece to Thomas Bartolini's *Anatomia reformata* is a horrible vision of the author's flayed skin seemingly hanging on the page (fig. IX.3).

But flaying as an artistic motif is much older than the mannerist period. It actually began with the Marsyas myth of the Greeks. The satyr Marsyas, son of Selene, the moon goddess, and Hyagnis, himself a satyr and a creature of Dionysus, is said to have been flayed alive against a tree on Apollo's orders. The reason for this horrible punishment was Marsyas's failure in a musical contest to which he had challenged Apollo. Apollo played his cithara and Marsyas the flute, but the result of the latter's playing was a veritable flaying of the hearer's ears. Marsyas's flaying was therefore the appropriate punishment to be meted out to him.

If we take the Marsyas myth in its literal sense, it appears to be a variation on the theme of punishment inflicted for artistic hubris. As such it is similar to the punishment imposed by Athena on the challenger Arachne after a tapestry-weaving contest: Arachne, as her name indicates, was turned into a spider. More important, the flaying of Marsyas can be read as an allegory of artistic creation, of artistic "possession" and the ultimate destruction of the artist by art. While Apollo *is* art, Marsyas's father, Hyagnis, as Dionysus's creature, is also art, in its Dionysiac aspects, and the flaying myth represents artistic creation as a self-flaying process.

Art as self-flaying: that is what is revealed by Marsyas's terrible scream in Ovid's *Metamorphoses:* "Quid me mihi detrahis?" ("Why do you tear me from my self?"). He who is possessed by the god of art cannot help inflicting upon his own self the horrible torture meted out to Marsyas.

Nietzsche, in *The Birth of Tragedy,* saw the artistic process as either Apollo-nian or Dionysiac. In his view Apollo was the god of art as pure subliminal delight while Dionysus was the god of art as the expression of sexual drives and pleasure in torture and *terribilità.* The Marsyas myth shows us that this is not so; there is no such dichotomy as described by Nietzsche that joins enlightened aesthetic pleasure to sexual passion in order to produce art. It appears that Apollo is as cruel as Marsyas; the two are fused into the person of the artist, a sadomasochistic couple of forces. The Dionysiac Marsyas enjoys being flayed as much as Apollo enjoys flaying him. Such is the terrible enjoyment of the creative artist, who feels the tearing off of his own self—even welcomes it—in the creative process.

One of the greatest artists to see himself as a Marsyas was Michelangelo. The artist who is possessed by the god of art, the Dionysiac person who is possessed by Apollo, must inflict upon himself the atrocious torment suffered by Marsyas: such a statement was made implicitly by Michelangelo in the *Last Judgment* fresco in the Sistine Chapel. It was made through the figure of his flayed Saint Bartholomew. Some of Michelangelo's contemporaries recognized Bartholomew as Marsyas. Aretino, Michelangelo's enemy, reproached the great prelates of the church who had commissioned the fresco for "preferring the flayed Marsyas to Saint Lawrence on his grill."[7] But it was not until 1925 that the Italian scholar La Cava recognized that the skin which the flayed Christian martyr Bartholomew holds in his hand (almost exactly in the center of the fresco) represents the features of the painter himself, of Michelangelo (fig. IX.4).[8]

We may infer that the scene had more than an edifying Christian function, that it also expressed a theory of art. It is both signature and aesthetic testament. Through Bartholomew this work tells us: "This fresco painted by Michelangelo is also the painter's own skin, the skin of his soul flayed alive by himself during the painting of his last great work."

In light of what we know about the personality of the great painter this interpretation of the Bartholomew figure does not seem too fantastic. A number of statements about self-alienation may be found in Michelangelo's sonnets, and some of the statements express a desire to be flayed alive. In a sonnet to his friend and admirer Cavalieri, for instance, Michelangelo offers

IX.4 Saint Bartholomew holding his own skin
with the features of Michelangelo; detail of
Last Judgment, Sistine Chapel.
Photo Vatican Museum; by permission.

his "mortal spoil" and "hairy skin" to beauty (that is, to the beauty of his
friend).[9] In another sonnet, in which Michelangelo speaks about "true virtue
that never changes even when one despoils it," the term he uses is *scorzzare*,
which means "pull off the bark, or skin."[10]

It is pertinent also to recall Michelangelo's theory about sculpture: that
stone carving is a flaying of the stone in order to discover the concept (*concetto*) hidden within it.[11] Long before the discovery of X rays, Michelangelo
formulated a theory of the haptic reading of inanimate matter. In the mannerist period, the idea of a concept or form hidden deep in nonorganic matter seems to have become almost universal. The painter and theorist Zuccari,
for example, spoke of the *idea interna* or *forma interna* to be found in things.[12]
Sculpture doubtlessly is a primarily haptic activity; yet in the late Renaissance and mannerist periods in which Michelangelo accomplished his last
artistic activities, these activities coincided with a theory of the transfer of
haptics to painting. Thus the vision of Michelangelo in his late period is a

vision in depth, like that of Zuccari and others. The Michelangelo skin which the flayed Bartholomew holds in his hand in the *Last Judgment* is a sign of this deep reading.

Flaying in Literature

The flaying motif is found in literature as well as in art. Walt Whitman was probably the first of the modern poets to view the body of man and woman haptically and to lay bare the features and lineaments of the homunculus within us—"this nucleus," as he calls it in his great ode to "the body electric."

> This is the female form.
> A divine nimbus exhales from it from head to foot. . . .
> Mad filaments, ungovernable shoots play out of it. . . .
> Hair, bosom, hips, bend of the legs, negligent falling
>   hands—all diffused . . . mine too diffused.
> Ebb stung by the flow, and the flow stung by the ebb. . . .
> Loveflesh swelling and deliciously aching.
> Limitless limpid jets of love hot and enormous. . . .
>   quivering jelly of love . . . white-blow and
>   delirious juice."[13]

Like the poets of expressionism but long before them, Whitman seeks to demolish the idea of the harmonious, the canon of neoclassical Greek symmetry. There is also in this demolition an exaltation: the glorification of America and what one might call the aesthetics of the machine. Mastering the machine and inventing new machines are the great American occupations of the time. But the body is also a machine. The inventors are only cyberneticians who make models of the human body with steel and steam.

Whitman's laying bare of the mechanics in us may also have a political purpose. Whitman was engaged body and soul in the fight against slavery, in the fight of the Union against the South. He saw slavery not only as a fight against a hateful form of exploitation of man by man but as a negation of the universality of man. Exploring the body deeper than the epidermis, therefore, was for him showing this deep universality. At this level, there are no whites or blacks, and it is this deep level which reveals us as what we truly are, conglomerates of nerves, muscles, and blood.[14] The idea of torture or self-torture seems to be absent from Whitman's poem. Flaying, the view in depth, is put at the service of generous egalitarian ideas.

Did this scanning in depth of the body imply a theory of scanning? Is there a hermeneutic theory of depth reading in Walt Whitman's work? The answer, I think, must be in the affirmative. One may speak, in Whitman's case, of social hermeneutics which rest on a haptic vision of things. This comes strongly to the fore in the 1871 pamphlet *Democratic Vistas* and in his numerous writings on the soldiers' hospitals of the Civil War. In the first-mentioned writing, he sees himself, long before the hero of Kafka's *Castle*, as a "surveyor" exploring Democracy in its "embryo condition."[15]

He also expounds his doctrine of personalism in terms that remind one strongly of his "body electric": the young American of the future should be "clear-blooded, strong-fibered," proud of his "stores of cephalic knowledge."[16] Literary creation, too, should be in depth: the writer who describes an American landscape, the poet who writes an ode to this landscape, Whitman says, should also take into account "the whole orb, with its geologic history": "I do not mean the smooth walks, trimmed hedges, posys and nightingales of the English poets. . . ."[17]

Finally, "the body electric"—but maimed, blood-soaked, pitiful—was also the body of America lying dissected on the operation tables of the Civil War: "The Marrow of the tragedy," Whitman writes, "concentrated in those Army Hospitals—(it seem'd sometimes as if the whole interest of the land, North and South, was one vast central hospital, and all the rest of the affair but flanges). . . ."[18]

The flaying motif is particularly vivid in the writings of Kafka. *In the Penal Colony* features a character called the Officer who is the inventor of a sort of flaying machine for punishing unruly military personnel. A half-naked prisoner is strapped into it and a needle is activated; it inscribes in the living flesh of the condemned man the text of the verdict imposed by the disciplinary regulation. The punishment machine is a textual machine; it prints a text on the skin of a living person (used, as it were, as a parchment). At the end of the story, the punishing turns out to be a form of self-punishing when the Author (that is, the inventor of the machine) straps himself into his own contraption and activates the mechanism.

Kafka did not content himself with the merely textual description of his machine. A letter sent to Milena Jesenka long after he wrote the story contains a sketch of a contraption very similar to the one in *Penal Colony:* a machine intended to literally split a man in two (fig. IX.5). Here is how Kafka describes it:

> I'm enclosing a drawing. These are four poles, through the two middle ones are driven rods to which the hands of the "delinquent" are fastened; through the two outer poles rods are driven for the feet. After the man has been bound in this way the rods are drawn slowly outwards until the man is torn apart in the middle. Against the post leans the inventor who, with crossed arms and legs, is giving himself great airs, as though the whole thing were his original invention, whereas he has only copied the butcher who stretches the disemboweled pig in his shop-front.[19]

Like the self-flaying of the man in Kokoschka's so-called Pietà, the quartering of the man in the drawing sent to Milena can be equated to a self-

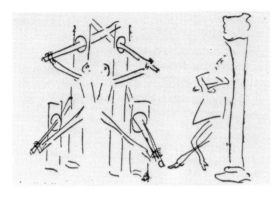

IX.5 Kafka's torture machine.
By permission of Schocken Books,
New York.

dismemberment. First, the person of the inventor in the drawing seems to be the mirror image of the man in the contraption; his crossed arms and legs correspond to those of the man in the machine. Second, the man in the machine corresponds almost exactly to the sketch of a man drawn on a postcard Kafka sent to his sister Ottla from the Scheselen sanatorium, where he was being treated for tuberculosis. In this picture, entitled "Ansichten aus meinem Leben" (View of my life), the man lies on his back on a table with outstretched limbs, just like the prisoner in the torture machine.[20]

Like Kokoschka, Kafka introduced into his marginal art—his doodles—the motif of the quartered and flayed creature as the symbol of an internal flaying. One thinks immediately of Baudelaire and the French decadents. "Je suis la plaie et le couteau / Je suis la victime et le bourreau," Baudelaire wrote ("I am the wound and the knife / I am the victim and the hangman"). Kafka is just as explicit. In one of his letters to Milena, written right after sending her the torture drawing, Kafka actually added: "Yes, torturing is extremely important to me: I am only preoccupied with torturing and being tortured."[21] Both doodles and reflection—and also the symbolic, anagogic content of *In the Penal Colony*—reveal Kafka's extraordinary understanding of the profoundly ambivalent and reversible nature of the artist, who is at once his own victim and his own executioner, at once flayer and flayed.

Kafka was perhaps alienated from men in the strange world of men, or from his father, or from this Milena he could not fully love; however that might have been, he knew as a certainty that as an artist he was also necessarily alienated from his own self; that he had to be. Thus his drawing is a representation of the universal *Selbstentfremdung* that is part of the being of the expressionist artist. His sketch is the sign of art as mortification of the flesh, the sign of the vision in depth that is expressionism. For Kafka as for Kokoschka—and for Michelangelo before them—to create a world of literary fiction or to paint a world was essentially to torture and to flay oneself.

Creation was tantamount to a process of extreme self-alienation; the depth vision was also a self-flaying.

Another *écorché*, another flayed muscleman of the expressionist period, hovers like a ghost in the background of Thomas Mann's *Magic Mountain*. In this novel, the human body appears suddenly hovering through the thin air before the eyes of the protagonist, Hans Castorp, like some sort of gelatinous transparency:

> It hovered before him, somewhere in space, remote from his grasp yet near his sense; this body, this opaquely whitish form giving out exhalations, moist, clammy; the skin with all its blemishes and native impurities, with its spots, pimples, discolorations, irregularities; its horny, scalelike regions covered over by soft streams and whorls of rudimentary lanugo. The acrid steaming shadows of the armpits corresponded in a mystic triangle to the pubic darkness, just as the eyes did to the red, epithelial mouth opening and the red blossoms of the breast to the navel lying perpendicularly below. Under the impulsion of a central organ and of the motor nerves originating in the spinal marrow, chest and abdomen functioned, the peritoneal cavity expanded and contracted, the breath, warmed and moistened by the mucous membrane of the respiratory canal, saturated with secretions, streamed out between the lips, after it had joined its oxygen to the hemoglobin of the blood in the air cells of the lungs.[22]

Later, in a sort of hymn to the human body—probably inspired by Whitman's "body electric"—Hans Castorp exclaims in French to his lover, Madame Chauchat: "Behold the marvelous symmetry of the human edifice . . . look at the spine as it descends toward the luxuriant doubleness of the buttocks and the huge branches of veins and nerves that pass from the torso into the limbs through the armpits. . . ."[23]

The doctors represented in the novel are described as X-ray fanatics. Behrens, the medical director of the sanatorium who paints as a hobby, speaks of the painter's craft in the following terms:

> If a man knows a bit about what goes on under the epidermis, that does no harm either. In other words, if he can paint a little below the surface, and stand in another relation to nature than just the lyrical, so to say: an artist who is a doctor, physiologist, and anatomist on the side, and has his own little way of thinking about the underside of things.[24]

Indicating the portrait of Madame Chauchat, his model and patient who is perhaps also his lover, Behrens goes on:

> That birthday suit there is painted with science. It is organically correct. You can examine it under the microscope. You can see not only the horny and mucous strata of the epidermis but I have suggested the texture of the corium underneath, with the oil and sweat glands, the blood vessels and tubercles—

and then under that still the layer of fat, the upholstering, you know, full of oil
ducts, the underpinning of the lovely female form. . . .[25]

Some of the characteristics of Behrens's style suggest that he is a sort of
expressionist painter. His canvases were

> all painted with a certain brisk dilettantism, the colors boldly dashed onto the
> canvas, and often looking as though they had been squeezed out of the tube.
> . . . There was too much red all over the face [of Madame Chauchat], the nose
> was badly out of drawing, the mouth was distorted.[26]

This passage suggests distortion techniques used by Kokoschka and Nolde
after the First World War. As one can see, Mann was far from being an
uncritical admirer of the *Bürgerschreck* style of the artists of his time; he also
understood the motivations behind their passionate search for the beautiful
ugliness or the ugly beauty of the flesh that is also meat, human meat.

In *The Magic Mountain* we find the same dialectical inversion between
aesthetics and science that was at the root of mannerism: the scientific description of the body gave way to expressionist aesthetics. The mediation
between the two aspects is done through a sort of medievalizing of aesthetics. The science-inspired glorification of the human body is followed by the
glorification of body destruction—the glorification of the flayed body—as
beneficial to the soul.

During a visit to the apartment of Naphta, the Jesuit and obscurantist
dialectician who provides a sort of counterweight to the "enlightened" peda-
gogue Settembrini, Hans Castorp is struck by a strange piece of sculpture
standing in a corner of a room:

> a pietà profoundly startling, artlessly effective to the point of being grotesque.
> The Madonna, in a cap, with gathered brows and wry, wailing mouth, with
> the Man of Sorrows on her lap. Considered as a work of art it was primitive
> and faulty, with crudely emphasized and ignorant anatomy, the hanging head
> bristling with thorns, face and limbs blood-besprinkled, great blobs of blood
> welling from the wound in the side and from the nail prints in hands and
> feet.[27]

Elsewhere I have identified this piece of sculpture as the so-called Röttgen
Pietà in the Landesmuseum in Bonn.[28] What is important in this introduction
of this horrifying piece of sculpture into the novel is its function. It helped
Mann develop and formulate in terms of medieval art the principal tenets of
expressionist aesthetics in words that neither Kokoschka nor Kafka would
have denied.

Recovering from the shock experienced at the sight of the pietà, Hans
Castorp declares: "I should never have thought there could be anything in
the world at once so—forgive me—so ugly, and so beautiful." Naphta
answers:

"All works of art whose function is to express the soul and the emotions of the soul . . . are always so ugly as to be beautiful, and so beautiful as to be ugly. That is a law. Their beauty is not fleshly beauty, which is merely insipid—but the beauty of the spirit. Moreover, physical beauty is an abstraction," he added; "only the inner beauty, the beauty of religious expression, has any actuality."[29]

Naphta makes it clear that his pietà belongs to the *signum mortificationis*. To him it is a glorification of the suffering of the flesh and the torture of the flesh as a principle which ensures the primacy of the spirit. The body is "absolutely insipid" (the expression in German, *das absolut Dumme*, is even stronger). For Naphta modern expressionist aesthetics are the translation of the main tenet of medieval Christian mystique concerning the inversed proportionality between body and soul: "The more the body blooms and blossoms, the more the soul withers and dries; but on the contrary, the more the body withers and dries, the more strongly the soul greens and grows."

When Naphta speaks of "creations that express . . . the beauty of the spirit," one is immediately reminded of Kandinsky's title *On the Spiritual in Art* and of his very similar propositions concerning artistic beauty. Like Naphta, Kandinsky demanded an art detached from the corporeal and expressing "the inner world of the soul and its emotions."

A second expressionist tenet comes to the fore in Naphta's discourse: the idea of the dialectical reversal between beauty and ugliness. The entire expressionist movement—Nolde, Barlach, Beckmann, Heckel, Kirchner, Kokoschka—was seeking to achieve the point of reversal where the ugly became the beautiful and the beautiful the ugly. Kokoschka's and Kafka's flayed bodies are perfect examples of this search for the ultimate point of reversal. These figures cannot be seen as a revival of the baroque Vanitas in which death is also present in one form or another. Kokoschka, Kafka, and Mann do not share the moralizing intentions of the baroque painters and writers. The flayed men of these three artists are allegories of the creative process itself. If they represent a sort of forced spiritualization of the human body—this "absolutely dumb" thing—this must be taken in the purely aesthetic sense of the phrase. As far as representation is concerned, Kokoschka, Kafka, and Mann could not accept the glorifying of the symmetrical and harmonious body of classical and neoclassical humanism. And the most radical means of spiritualizing the body at their disposal to make it cease to be "dumb" was the expressionist dismemberment and X-ray look, which made the sublime ugliness of the vital organs appear under the "imbecile beauty" of the surface, when the muscles and vessels and nerves became visible under the marmoreal and "classical" epidermis. It is in this sense, too, that the murderer is also a hope in Kokoschka's title. Kokoschka's youthful work, like the work of Kafka and Mann, was a "theater of cruelty" in advance of its time, and of the formula that was later to become fashionable.[30] Art was *mortificatio carnis*.

It is interesting to observe that Mann later became conscious of the dangers lurking in this sort of aesthetic sadism. In *Doctor Faustus*, begun during the dark hours of the Second World War, he makes his alter ego, the humanist Serenus Zeitblom, say about his narrative: "Here no one can follow me who has not as I have experienced in his very soul how near aestheticism and barbarism are to each other: aestheticism as the herald of barbarism."[31] Zeitblom is speaking of the art of his friend Leverkühn. Some lines later he adds: "What I have in mind is Leverkühn's preference for the glissando. Of course preference is not the right word; I only mean that at least in this work, *The Apocalypse*, he makes exceptionally frequent use of it." What Mann is saying here through Zeitblom is that those expressionist or dodecaphonist composers who raised the scream, the howl, to the level of stylistic device later would find it hard to avoid howling with the wolves around them.

Mann returned to this theme many times in the course of *Doctor Faustus*. His reproach may be reformulated thusly: the artist of the avant-garde who treated his medium sadistically, who "prepared barbarity in himself" (and it is obvious that he included himself as a writer in this barbaric avant-garde), merely practiced on the aesthetic level what the Nazis practiced on the human flesh. There is, of course, a great deal of difference between actual and aesthetic sadism. Yet Mann seems to have played down the difference.

We have here, once again, the theory of the stylistic parallelism between politics and art. Isaac Babel's theory on line and color (see chap. V) reappears here in another form. The danger of the creative technique through *mortificatio carnis* is that it becomes in the end *mortificatio artis*.

After Expressionism

Did the X-ray technique, the motif of the flayed man, survive expressionism? Can it be said, for instance, that it became a central theme of surrealism? This is by no means certain. What is foregrounded by surrealist art is the representation of human organs as severed from the body rather than an X-ray view of this body. This is the case in many works by Salvador Dali, Max Ernst, and others. The iconographic genealogy that preceded the painting of these limbs and organs severed from their bodies is to be seen in the votive images hung in churches near the portraits or statues of the healer saints, especially in Italy and Spain.[32] These ex-voto organs, usually made of solid wax, are placed there even today by the faithful in the hope that the saint will heal the actual organs designated by those signs or icons placed in full view. The influence of such votive images is certainly to be felt in Dali's pictures and in Buñuel's surrealist films—both of them being essentially Spanish in spite of their declared cosmopolitanism.[33]

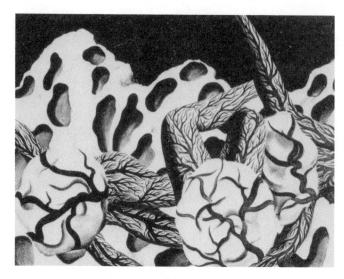

IX.6 *The Blood of the World* by Magritte.
Copyright C. Herscovici/ARS N.Y., 1989; by permission.

Yet, at the time, the motif of the flayed man sometimes reappeared. It is found, for example, in Dali's *Lugubrious Game*, which shows entrails and nerves cascading out of the human envelope.[34] Similarly, *Premonition of the Civil War*[35] and *Autumn Cannibalism*[36] show an organism in the process of eating its own organs. In all these pictures the allegorical content does not concern individual destiny but a political situation. Dali himself said that he had planned to paint a body devouring itself as an allegory of the Spanish Civil War.

Another painter who frequently represented the bleeding skinless anatomy is René Magritte. His *Blood of the World* presents a flayed woman's legs (fig. IX.6).[37] This suggests that another source of this surrealist carving up of the human body, especially of the female body, is probably to be found in the writings of the Marquis de Sade. Didn't André Breton write that "Sade was a surrealist in his sadism"? Most of the members of the surrealist group exalted the techniques of Sade, whose game with the human body taken as a sort of sexual doll seemed to them to be endowed with a liberating force. Thus the dolls of Hans Bellmer, dissected, raped, dislocated, are the result of this *imitatio Sadis*. In Bellmer's *Blood-Stained Roses* of 1950, the female genitals are replaced by blood-dripping petals.[38]

Hundreds of descriptions of cut and bleeding organs may be found in surrealist literature. But many of them were introduced by the surrealists not as examples of the possibilities offered by a new haptic vision but as metaphors of language. Thus the slitting of a woman's eye in Buñuel's film *Un Chien Andalou* is a cosmic metaphor: a cloud cuts off the brilliance of the moon's surface just as one might cut off a woman's eye with a razor blade. Similarly, the severed and roaming hand in *The Exterminating Angel* is a vectorial component which signifies the optical character of the type of vision that is necessary to read this film.

What surrealism has in common with sixteenth-century mannerism is precisely the atmosphere of anesthetized emotions in the face of cruelty and pain. For both, playing with dissected limbs was an aesthetic game.[39]

The last author to be inscribed at the end of the line of writers who exalted the *écorché* beneath the skin of woman is Vladimir Nabokov, or at least his somber hero Humbert Humbert. *Lolita* is full of literary allusions, such as this passage in which Humbert describes his amorously cannibalistic desires:

> And I was such a friend, such a passionate father, such a good pediatrician attending to all the wants of my little auburn brunette. My only grudge against nature was that I could not turn my Lolita inside out and apply voracious lips to her young matrix, her unknown heart, her nacreous liver, the seagrapes of her lungs, her comely twin kidneys. . . .[40]

There can be no doubt whatsoever that it is through the regard of Whitman and Mann that Nabokov viewed the body of his imaginary nymphette.

Still another artist belongs in our exhibit. It was in the Berlin of 1927 and 1928, where Francis Bacon tried to learn his craft, that he was exposed to the postexpressionist or Neue Sachlichkeit (New Objectivity) atmosphere. After he had become rich and famous, many of the interviews the painter gave echoed the excitement of this early period to the extent that some of them may be regarded as expressionist professions of faith. Thus, speaking of Matthias Grünewald, the model par excellence of German expressionism, Bacon declared:

> Can you call the famous Isenheimer altar [see fig. II.9] a horror piece? It's one of the greatest paintings of the crucifixion, with the body studded with thorns like nails, but oddly enough, the form is so grand it takes away from the horror. But that is grand horror in the sense that it is so vitalizing, isn't it; isn't that how people came out of the great tragedies of Greece, the Agamemnon. . . .[41]

Another expressionist attitude of Bacon's is his obsession with the representation of screams. Isn't Edvard Munch's *Scream* the archexpressionist painting? As Bacon said:

> I wanted to paint the scream more than the horror. And I think that if I had really thought about what causes somebody to scream—the horror that produces a scream—it would have made the screams I tried to paint more successful. . . .I like, you may say, the glitter and color that comes from the mouth, and I've always in a sense wanted to be able to paint the mouth like Monet painted a sunset. But I've never succeeded in doing it. But I was also

very influenced by what I saw before I began to paint—the Eisenstein film *Battleship Potemkin* and the Odessa steppe sequence in which there is this wonderful shot of the nurse screaming. Also when I first went to Paris, I found in an old bookshop a book on diseases of the mouth which had beautiful hand-colored plates, and it had a tremendous effect on me.[42]

It is interesting to observe that one source of Bacon's inspiration—like that of Kokoschka—was the reading of books about medical pathology. In passages that follow this description of his encounter with old medical treatises, Bacon also mentions a work which had a considerable influence on him: *Positioning in Radiography* by K. C. Clark. Again X-ray vision was used as a model of vision for depicting human beings.

Bacon's attitude toward his own medium is violent, like that of the expressionsts and the Neue Sachlichkeit painters. He too describes the art of painting as a kind of murder and torture of the medium:

> My models inhibit me because I like them. I don't want to practise the injury that I do to them in my work before them. I would rather practise the injury in private by which I think I can record the facts of them more clearly.[43]

It must be emphasized that Bacon is not speaking of violence against his models but of the sublimation of this violence that is converted into violence toward the canvas and the picture itself.

What was the philosophical justification for such violence? Responding to an interviewer's question as to why the theme of the crucifixion is so intimately bound up in his painting with images of the butcher's block, Bacon declared: "We are meat, we are potential carcasses. If I go into a butcher's shop I always think it is surprising that I wasn't there instead of the animal." And he reminded his interviewer of the terrible beauty of dead flesh: "One has got to remember as a painter that there is this great beauty of the color of meat."[44]

It is fascinating to imagine Bacon roaming the motorways in search of this "terrible beauty," the expressionist beauty of death on the road:

> In all the motor accidents I have seen, people strewn across the road, the first thing you think of is the strange beauty, the vision of it, before you think of trying to do anything. It's to do with the unusualness of it. I once saw a bad car accident on a large road, and the bodies were strewn about with broken glass from the car, and the blood and various possessions, and it was in fact very beautiful. I think the beauty in it is terribly elusive, but it just happened to be in the disposition of the bodies, the way they lay and the blood, and perhaps it was also because it was not a thing one was used to seeing. . . . It was midday, when the sun was very strong and on a white road.[45]

Bacon's very special expressionism is an expressionism that has been colored by the existentialist age and has acquired something of the existentialist spirit. His aim is to show the concrete reality of the bleeding body-meat as the ultimate and terrible beauty of nothingness itself—to which, the painter ceaselessly tells us, we are ineluctably promised.

The Mexican Tradition

Another great tradition, the Mexican, had a flayed figure among its pantheon of gods: Xipe-Totec, *nuestro Señor el desollado* (our Lord the flayed being). Modern Mexican art and literature have revived the Xipe-Totec motif and transferred images of the terrible ritual to the textual and visual domains.

One great novel of modern Latin-American literature explicitly presents itself as a theory of reading or scanning as a sort of hermeneutics through haptics. This is Salvador Elizondo's *Faraboeuf.* The cover of the first Mexican paperback edition of the book, incidentally, shows a red diagram which seems to represent the cross-section of a human epidermis.[46]

Moreover, in the middle of the novel we find "Directions for Use" of the product—that is, the novel:

> When you read this book: start from right to left. . . . Start with the left side of the foot . . . continue till you reach the right face of the limb while bearing in mind all the time that the words on the right and on the left are addressed to the operator and not to the person that is operated on.
>
> Subsequently: slit [the skin] from left to right . . . start with the left side of the foot. . . . Continue toward the right face of the limb. . . .[47]

What is implied here is that the reading process is like a flaying done by the reader, like the opening of a slit in the living flesh of the text. A drawing accompanies the "Directions" (fig. IX.7). This picture recurs three times in this middle chapter.[48]

The chapter that follows is the description of a torture scene:

> Things proceed in the following manner: from the first moment [of the slitting of the skin] the blood begins to drip down along the folds in his body, rolling like zebra stripes on the distorted skin, rolling like thin scarlet threads that divide like stars around the sex of the saint—the only part of his body which under such conditions has remained untouched; finally they accumulate in the pubic parts until blood at last begins to drip down again onto the pavement this time, and remain there for a few moments as it turns black as coal. . . .[49]

It is difficult to say whether the scene described here is that of an actual torture. There are indications that it is the description of a Chinese torture the novelist saw in photographic reproduction in an old magazine. But we know from the "Directions for Use" that the novelist is also speaking of our reading activity.

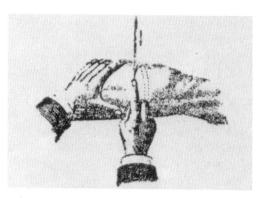

IX.7 Drawing from Salvador Elizondo's *Faraboeuf.*
By permission of Joaquin Mortiz, Mexico City.

Nor are allusions to self-flaying lacking in Elizondo's novel. This is the
sense of a question asked by the narrator, Faraboeuf:

> You think, perhaps, that you are prey of an hallucination? Is it possible that
> you should be so confused? This man hanging mutilated from a scaffold
> bathed in his own blood, is he not you? Could it be that an enormous mirror
> were hanging right here . . .?[50]

Elizondo's novel, as a matter of fact, must be inscribed in the Mexican
tradition of the flayed god. It is a tradition that I left aside in the first part of
this chapter, where I concentrated rather heavily on the Western tradition.
Xipe-Totec, the god of renewal, the Mexican homunculus, was represented
with his new skin hanging over his shoulders. He was not only a god of
death and suffering but also of spring, dance, and flowers. And yet horrible
sacrifices were made in his name. Frazer, George Kubler, and others have
described the human sacrifices to this god, in which young men were seized
in the fields they were tilling and flayed alive, their skins tied like togas
around the shoulders of the Xipe-Totec statues.[51]

I have already noted that modern Mexican artists often describe the heroes
of the revolution in terms of a revival of this horrible sacrifice. A case in
point is that of the painter Arnold Belkin, who sees the Mexican Revolution
as a meeting place for *écorchés* (fig. IX.8).

Being flayed sometimes becomes the expression of personal anguish more
than of historical fate. This is the case with the artist Frida Kahlo. As a girl,
Kahlo was run over by a bus in Mexico City and a metal bar impaled her,
damaging her womb and spine. It was only later, perhaps under the impact
of her encounter with painting through the agency of her husband, the
muralist Diego Rivera, that she gave pictorial expression to this very real
memory of torture. Yet there is more than just the wish to evoke private
suffering in Kahlo's *Two Fridas*, in which she has represented herself and her

IX.8 Detail of *Betrayal and Death of Zapata* by Arnold Belkin.
Collection Centro Cultural Wilfredo Lam, Havana; by permission of the artist.

double with their hearts torn out of their breasts and bleeding on their white dresses. This picture may be taken to symbolize mental suffering, the pains of the heart. But beyond that, Kahlo must have meant to inscribe herself in the cultural tradition of her land, in the Xipe-Totec tradition. The artist must suffer, must dissect herself, as Kahlo does: she holds in her hands the surgical scissors.

Like Dionysus and Apollo, Xipe-Totec was an ambiguous god of suffering and creation—and of creation through suffering and self-torture. It is in this allegory of creation, more than in anything else, perhaps, that, in John Donne's phrase, "East meets West."

Below the Surface

Extreme haptics is a sign of extreme liminality and, in the first place, of the extreme liminality of a period. Indeed, Michelangelo produced his flayed bodies at a time of crisis: when Italy, shattered by the sack of Rome, was becoming more and more manneristic in its aesthetic ideals, and when the extreme opticity of the Renaissance was no longer regarded as compulsory by many artists. Similarly, German expressionism was a symptom of the liminality of the artistic condition in the Europe of the imperialist era. Sacher-Masoch was the expression of this period when the alienated artist saw his craft as a sort of masochistic self-crucifixion or *écorchement*. The artist in extremis, to paraphrase Walter Sokel, saw himself as a man in a limit situation, on the verge of his own desegregation, just as the surrounding world was also liable, at any moment, to break the limits of selfhood and penetrate or violate the self.

At the same time, the map of Europe—this outer skin of the artist's home—was seen as a map about to "peel off" and expose "the works" (be they those of imperialism, nationalism, or capitalism). In present-day Mexico, artists and writers have internalized the terrible ritual of the wrenching out of human hearts as a means of appeasing the gods. Their art is a symptom of the urgency of the situation. When will these gods demand that the map skin of the country be split open and rolled off the dermic earth?

Extreme hapticity, as noted in the preceding chapter, is also a sign of transfer, and of a transfer reversal. In the case of Michelangelo, the violence of wrenching open the stone in order to extract the *concetto* was transferred to the self, and the artist saw himself as a Marsyas. In our century this transfer has been reversed, and the violence felt in the self is done to the medium, to the skin of the medium, that is, to the canvas or the paper pasted on the canvas. In many cases so-called landscape art resembles the strip mining it may have consciously imitated: a splitting of the earth's "skin." And conversely, as we shall see in the next chapter, it is haptic qualities that are demanded of the present-day observer, whom we might call a "deconstructionist spectator": to probe with one's eyes not the surface but the texture, and beneath the texture.

X

PEELING OFF SKINS

In the preceding chapter we saw the anagogic aspects of the Marsyas myth: how the flaying of Marsyas may be construed as a description of the deeper level of the creative process, the struggle of antithetical forces—the Apollonian and the Dionysiac—in one and the same pulsion toward art. In the present chapter the allegorical, metaliterary aspects of the same myth will be examined.

From the Renaissance onward, the torture of Marsyas by Apollo served symbolic purposes. Thus the anatomist Vesalius used the motif to adorn the initial letter V on one page of the 1543 edition of his great *De humanis corpore fabrica*, signifying that he, the surgeon, the V behind the illustration, was a victor over the cadaver he had set out to dissect. Indeed, Vesalius's *Fabrica* is generally considered to contain the first truly scientific description of the human body. V also signified the final victory of modern anatomy over the old Galenist school. Vesalius was an Apollo tearing off the skin of the human body to let us see the true functioning of the organs beneath it.[1]

About a century later, in 1634, the Jesuit Father Claude François Ménestrier featured a picture of Apollo flaying Marsyas in his authoritative *L'art des emblèmes*, which bears the long subtitle *où s'enseigne la morale par les figures de la fable, de l'histoire, et de la nature*.[2] Ménestrier commented that he had used the picture "to teach those who are wont to read Fables and the inventions of Poetry, lest they should stop at these fictions, which are but as the bark of many philosophical truths." Thus Apollo, the god of poetry, was painted in the act of flaying Marsyas precisely "to teach the proper way to skin the Fables, that is, to discover the meaning that they contain."[3]

I have been unable to find a similar hermeneutic interpretation of the flaying of Marsyas in other authors of the period—that is, in the very rich literature of emblems and emblematics of the late baroque, from the sixteenth century onward. Yet Ménestrier must have been familiar with other works in which this meta-artistic interpretation of the myth is present. Edgard Wind, the modern discoverer of the anagogic importance of the Marsyas myth, mentioned that "in the drunken speech of Alcibiades [in the *Symposium*] Socrates himself was called a Marsyas." And, Wind continued:

That Socrates, who was a disciple of Apollo and had adopted from an inscription on Apollo's temple at Delphi his own maxim "Know thyself," should be figuratively described as a Silenus and a Marsyas meant that this ruthless pursuit of bewildering questions was but the disguise of an inward clarity—a disguise which was indispensable because it reckoned with the twofold nature of man. To bring out the hidden clarity . . . required a Cathartic method, a Dionysian ordeal by which the "terrestrial Marsyas" was tortured so that the "heavenly Apollo" might be crowned.[4]

The metaliterary interpretation of Ménestrier smacks of mannerist Neoplatonism. As noted in chapter IX, Michelangelo's mannerist view of himself as a sculptor who flayed layer upon layer of stone until the *concetto* hidden inside it finally appeared must have predisposed him to signing his doomsday fresco with his own flayed skin. But perhaps what inspired Ménestrier was not Neoplatonist doctrine but rather the layer upon layer of meaning that defined the Christian exegetical tradition. In this tradition the Scripture, the holy text, was but the crystallization of four semantic strata: the literal, the allegorical, the homiletic, and the anagogic.[5] Penetrating to the most secret, the anagogic, meaning certainly meant shedding—perhaps through flaying—stratum after stratum of textual interpretation.[6]

The Jewish tradition knew the same categories, respectively called *pshat*, *remez*, *drash*, and *sod*. The word *lifshot* (hence *pshat*), which is used to designate the first layer of interpretation, may mean to undress or sometimes to flay (as in the expression *lifshot-or*). Thus several researchers have shown that even the first layer of interpretation is in reality the result of a laying bare, an undressing or flaying.[7] There are, of course, no satyrs and therefore no Marsyas in the Mosaic tradition. Yet there is a sort of Jewish Saint Bartholomew: Akiba, the first-century zealot, rabbi, and Bible exegete who threw in his lot with the anti-Roman rebel Bar-Kokhba and is said to have been captured and flayed alive by the Romans. The punishment seems to have been intended to correspond to his lifetime activity as a flayer of texts.

A curious anti-Christian haggadah, or legend, is related by Louis Ginzberg.[8] It tells how Jesus became master of the Divine Name, the ineffable Name of God whose possession enables the possessor to accomplish miracles:

> Since the knowledge of the Divine Name enabled anyone to accomplish all one desired, a device was necessary to prevent misuse. At the gate of the temple, two brazen dogs were placed so that whenever a person who had acquired the knowledge of the Name would pass, they began to bark. Frightened by this sound, the person would forget the knowledge of the Name. Jesus, however, had written the Name on a paper, which he hid under his skin.

Thus Jesus was said to have been a sort of self-flayer for the purpose of inscribing the holiest of texts under his skin. The legend turns him into a sort of prefiguration of the Officer in Kafka's *Penal Colony* (see chap. IX).

In some of the works analyzed in the preceding chapter, the flaying theme has metapictorial or metatextual aspects.[9] The art works and the stories tell us that they should be read as one dissects a body. This is certainly true of Michelangelo's "signature" in the *Last Judgment* fresco and of Kokoschka's self-flayed image. As for Kafka's torture machine, it is used not only as a description of the self-alienating creative process that characterizes all genuinely artistic activity but also to demonstrate the existence of a specific theory of reading. In other words, it is another version of the metaphor used by hermeneuticians: textual reading is the shedding of layer after layer of text, just as one peels an onion. Kafka thus follows in the footsteps of Ménestrier, though in Kafka's case, as in the cases of Kokoschka and Michelangelo, the onion is not mythical but is a human body, the body of the writer himself.

Pictures as Skins

In the baroque age, a few years before Ménestrier produced his interpretation of Marsyas, a Dutch draftsman, Dionysus Padtbrugge, saw the production of maps as a sort of skinning of the earth globe (fig. X.1). His drawing depicts the great Swedish cartographer Olaf Rudbeck "flanked by ancient authorities" as he "anatomizes the map of Scandinavia in search of Atlantis." It was used by Rudbeck as the frontispiece for his book *Atlantica* in 1675.[10]

What is significant is the use of the word *anatomizes*, which shows that the cartographer saw himself as a surgeon, a flayer of the earth. This metaphor at the front of Rudbeck's book must have struck the imagination of the common reader, who saw the physician or surgeon as the man of science par excellence and must have had some difficulty understanding the map's Mercator projection. This picture-metaphor conceals the approximate character of the projection, which, like all projections of a round surface over a flat one, was unable to square the circle in a perfect manner. Behind it lurks a specific ideology, the one that sees the map of the kingdom as the double of the king's body.

Another skin metaphor in art is that of the palimpsest. According to this metaphor, behind the epidermic skin of a painting there may be a dermic layer that can be brought to the fore by the rolling up or down of the first skin. This is the theme of a painting of the holy family attributed to Angolo del Moro (fig. X.2). The Magrittian idea that the canvas is but a sort of epidermic layer of reality—expressed in Magritte's *La condition humaine* and *Les promenades d'Euclide*[11] and by other Belgian painters—is here prefigured.

In the case of Magritte, one may wonder whether the idea of the canvas as skin serves to glorify a neo-Aristotelian concept of relative or absolute mimesis or whether it is used to debunk that concept. There are some Magritte paintings, such as *Le soir qui tombe*, in which the peeling or "falling" sky

X.1 Cartographer Olof Rudbeck, surrounded
by allegorical figures, "anatomizes" the map
of the earth. From Rudbeck's *Atlantica*,
Uppsala, editio princeps, 1675.
Photo Haifa University Library; by permission.

reveals not a layer of reality but only emptiness.[12] Not so here: the permanence of the vision of the holy family is confirmed by the underlayer, as
though the artist meant to tell us that his picture is merely the imprint of a
cosmic reality. Moreover, the skin idea extends even to the artist's signature:
the *cartellino* that bears the signature also seems to be peeling off the canvas.

The essential emptiness behind figurative representation is hinted at,
however, in a picture of about the same period, a *Vanitas* by the seventeenth-century painter Jean François de la Motte (fig. X.3).[13] As suggested by
the scarcely visible title, *Cogitas Mori*, inscribed on the peeling-off canvas, it
is a memento mori. One suspects that the painter was a sympathizer of
Jansenism, the religious movement that emphasized the emptiness of human
life and the vanity of representation itself.

In the surrealist period one finds the *Portrait of Gala* by Max Ernst peeling
away from the background as a poster from a wall.[14] As it falls off, the image

X.2 *A Vision of the Holy Family near Verona,* attributed to
Battista Angolo del Moro, 1581.
*Photo Allen Memorial Art Museum, Oberlin College,
Oberlin, Ohio; by permission.*

curls and reveals a cosmic sky with huge stars and moons behind it. The
portrait was probably painted around 1925; Gala, Paul Eluard's wife, had
just added Ernst to her list of conquests. Perhaps the young painter already
felt that the woman was detaching herself from him, leaving him with a
terrible and empty cosmos as a parting gift.

This idea of the empty cosmic sky peeling away was presented in a cognate form long before Ernst set about painting his *Portrait of Gala.* A detail of
Giotto's *Last Judgment* in the Scrovegni Chapel in Padua shows an angel
rolling up the sky to reveal the *terribilità* of the divine abode from which the
very cosmos emanates (fig. X.4). The glorious abode of God behind the angel
looks very much like a leather and wood Bible cover, inset with diamonds.
Thus the sky seems the emanation of the celestial architecture, that is, the
Bible.

One does not need to wonder whether cabalistic ideas colored the pure
Roman Catholic faith of Giotto. He painted in the fourteenth century,
when the Cabala had not yet penetrated the Christian sphere. Nevertheless, one of its central ideas, that the cosmos was constituted after the
blueprint that was the text of the Law, of the Scripture, is very much a
part of New Testament theology. The idea that God is essentially logos
and that the alpha and omega are the beginning and end of everything
was clearly voiced in the Gospels. The idea that the visible world is preg-

X.3 *Vanitas* by Jean François de la Motte.
*Author's photograph; by permission of the
Musée des Beaux Arts, Dijon.*

nant with language, having been impregnated with it from the beginning,
is expressed here in Giotto's curious vision of the vault of the sky being
unrolled over the cosmos.

The canvas as skin is not always peeling off its stretcher. The American
artist Jasper Johns, for example, used his canvases as substitute skins. The
artist obtained these "skins" by rubbing his own face and body in colored
oils and then rubbing them against sheets of paper or canvas. They are
veritable haptic creations, less deep (or more superficial) than the attempts at
X-ray painting that characterized the beginnings of German expressionism.[15]

The idea of painting as a palimpsest or substitute skin for the artist coex-
ists, in the second half of the twentieth century, with that of the painting as
a violated and sliced skin. I am referring to the Italian painter Fontana, with
his many sliced and mutilated canvases. If one confronts these canvases with
the sixteenth-century pagan and mannerist Marsyas, everything points to a
transfer. It is as though the Marsyas theme had suddenly left the canvases
on which it was represented (had peeled away, as it were) in order to turn
the painter into a raging Apollo. From being a canonized subject, the flaying
of Marsyas has become a technique, and the canvas itself has become a
Marsyaslike skin under the hand of the violent modern painter. To paraphrase Kokoschka, murder has become the hope of painters. A decisive step

X.4 Detail of fresco by Giotto in the
Scrovegni Chapel, Padua.
Author's photograph.

in this transfer of violence was taken by action painting, the abstract expressionist movement. With Jackson Pollock and other members of this group, the violence of the painter dances, his jets of splashing paint becoming themselves the subject of the work, exactly as the flaying violence of the razor became the subject of Fontana.

In the course of history a great deal of violence has been unleashed against pictures. There was Byzantine iconoclasm, the Jewish and Christian destruction of idols, the *Bilderstürme* organized by Protestants against pictures of the Virgin and the Catholic saints, and many more such onslaughts. But only in our century has violence become endowed with a constitutive—one is tempted to say creative—aspect, where the destruction of an icon becomes tantamount to its creation.

Needless to say, political journalism has availed itself of this modern pictorial sadism to depict graphically the lot of fallen idols and fallen tyrants, or sometimes to prophesy their fall. Thus a French magazine, *L'Evènement du Jeudi,* described the end of the Stroessner regime in Paraguay by showing a large photograph of General Stroessner peeling off a wall in Montevideo,[16]

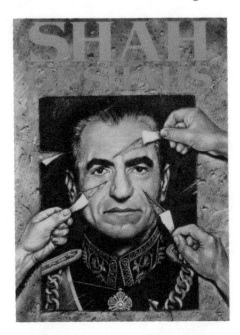

X.5 The Shah of Iran as a torn-off poster.
Cover design for Ryszard Kapuscinski,
Shah of Shahs (Vintage Books, 1986).
By permission of Random House, New York.

and a book on the fall of the Shah of Iran showed a symbolic skinning of his
portrait on the walls of Tehran (fig. X.5).

Almost a half-century before the shah's pictorial skinning, Arthur Koestler
had his arch-Stalinist commissar Ivanov, one of the protagonists of *Darkness
at Noon,* use the skin metaphor: "We are tearing the old skin off mankind
and giving it a new one. That is not an occupation for people with weak
nerves." And the deviationist Rubashov retorts: "You call it vivisection mo-
rality. To me it sometimes seems as though the experimenters had torn the
skin off the victim and left it standing with bared tissues, muscles and
nerves. . . ."[17]

Now we return to the theme of the first illustration in this chapter. Literature as cartography was a favorite subject with Jorge Luis Borges. Actually,
the idea of the map as the skin of the universe or at least the skin of the
kingdom, as shown in figure X.1, is also the theme of Borges's short story
"On the Strictness of Science." In it Borges wrote:

> In those days, the Art of Cartography attained such Perfection that the map of
> one single Province extended over a whole City, and the map of the empire, a
> whole Province. As time went by, those Immense Maps did not please any
> longer and the Colleges of Cartography erected a Map of the Empire that had

the same size as the Empire and coincided with it point by point. Being less interested in Cartography than the previous ones, the Subsequent Generations deemed this cumbersome Map useless, and— not without impiety—they entrusted it to the inclemencies of the Sun and Winters. In the deserts of the East there subsist still dilapidated ruins of the Map, inhabited by Beasts and Beggars; in all the rest of the Country, there are not to be found any other relics of the Geographical Disciplines.[18]

In his own erudite or pseudo-erudite way, Borges mocks the idea of an equation between the body of the king and the geography of the nation, the idea of the king's two bodies—no matter whether the king is an actual one or merely a Latin-American dictator. It is under the banner of this idea that so many bloody wars have been fought.

Texts as Skins

How did the idea of the text as palimpsest fare in literature? One important landmark toward the palimpsest texts of the twentieth century is *Katers Murr* by E. T. A. Hoffmann.[19] In this novel the "autobiography" of the hero, the composer Johannes Kreisler, alternates with the "opinions on life" which his cat, Murr, "scratched" between the lines of the "autobiography." In writing a novel beneath the surface, as it were, of another novel, Hoffmann may have been guided by an idea expressed by his mentor Friedrich Schlegel, that the ideal form of the novel had to include a theory of the novel. Indeed, a palimpsest such as *Murr* implies a theory of the text as essentially multilayered, polysemic, and ambiguous.

Among present-day literary products, the one that most resembles a palimpsest is Raymond Queneau's *Cent mille milliards de poèmes,* which is made up of movable strips of paper on which lines are inscribed; these strips may be combined any way one chooses. The period in which Queneau composed this "book," the late 1950s and early 1960s, was one in which a number of Parisian painters created pictures by tearing off strips of posters previously pasted on canvas or by transferring whole sections of peeling-off walls to their canvases.

Yet the direct heirs to Ménestrier are to be found in the sphere of literary theory. Gérard Genette, in his *Palimpsestes,* explicitly refers to the various layers of text that have to be "torn off" in order for the palimpsest text (the architext or hypertext) to appear.[20] These layers are the intertext, the metatext, and the paratext. The palimpsest text, or architext, is of course the ultimate text, the one most pregnant with meaning. It is Genette who has come closest to performing an Apollonian flaying of the text.

But it is Derrida and his deconstructionist endeavor that have come closest to a Dionysian flaunting of the text as "skin"—like the skins, or *pharmakoi,* that the ancient Greeks wrapped themselves in to sweep across the streets of a contaminated city. Essentially haptic qualities are demanded of the deconstructionist performer, spectator, and reader; not to follow optically the "line of ideas" in a text or in a picture and see only the representation proper, the surface, but to probe with the eyes the pictorial texture and even to enter the texture and probe below the texture. On the textual level, deconstructionist reading explores the clefts and crevices in the text, what Derrida called the *aporia* in the text; and beneath the textual surface, what counts is not the ostensible textual "content" but the aporetic texture in which this "content" is enveloped. For Derrida, it is the *logos* as typographical skin and texture that is the true *logos*, and not the opticality of the ideas it presents. The process implicity advocated by Derrida and his school is actually the opposite to that advocated by Genette (and before him by Ingarden): there is no *aletheia*. No hypothetical palimpsest text is made to appear through the tearing off of scraps of textual skins; the text itself, in its skinlike aspect, is the thing. What you see through a haptical apprehension of the text is what you get. The object of deconstructionist investigations is the skin text. Deconstructionists are adventurers in the skin trade.

XI

READING ORDER AND DISORDER

During the past decade, several articles and books have been devoted to the concepts of entropy, randomness, and noise in works of art, especially in visual works of art.[1] The present chapter is therefore but a footnote to this series of often brilliant studies on the subject. Its aim is to examine the question of parallelism between textual and visual art works from the point of view of the order/disorder dichotomy—specifically, entropy versus order or randomness and noise versus order.

The visual work of art constitutes the point of departure of this examination because it is, for me, the privileged locus of the dialectical process that links the two poles of the dichotomy. In a second stage I will examine these same poles in the context of literature.

The development of Western art seems to point toward an ever greater awareness by artists of the centrality of this dichotomy, an awareness that manifests in the art work itself, so that the real subject of the work becomes this dialectic relation. This consciousness is expressed explicitly in one modern movement, concrete poetry, which we will look at later in this chapter.

Ocular Proximity

Every piece of sculpture or painting, even one that is placed under the aegis of a strict aesthetic order—be it the strictest of classical or neoclassical masterpieces—offers a chaotic aspect to the eye if viewed at a close or microscopic level. Any observer of these so-called harmonious or polished pieces needs only to draw near the bronze or marble surfaces of the sculptures or, in terms of painting, near the glossy surfaces of the Renaissance canvases to notice that what appeared smooth and orderly is in reality a sort of granulous lunar landscape or a maze of irregular microblots.

Such disorder is but the disorder of what the Greeks called *hylē*, matter itself. This disorder was contrasted to *morphē*, the form imposed upon matter. E. H. Gombrich has described this matter/form dichotomy in terms of the "canvas versus nature" game; in creating their works, artists swing forever back and forth between nature as orderly representation and their canvases as the microscopic disorder of paint and pigment.[2]

From another perspective, one might say that so-called classical aesthetics rejects the proximity of the eye, rejects proximity altogether, because the structural identity of the object that is described or referred to disappears under the scrutiny of microscopic examination. The physical analogon[3] to this object in the marble or on the stretched canvas reveals an essential disorder that runs counter to the aesthetic premises of classical creation—an order that cannot be mastered.

Nevertheless, there were at least two important exceptions to this rule concerning the rejection of proximity as a dangerous, chaos-revealing device during the Renaissance: the genre of the anamorphose and the stylistic modality of the unfinished, the *non finito*.

The word *anamorphose* comes from the Greek *ana* ("again") and *morphē*. This type of drawing or painting, "reconstituted form," implies a proximity of the eye, if not to the actual canvas at least to the plane surface in which the canvas is inscribed. Indeed, an anamorphose cannot be reconstituted or reconstructed unless the eye sees the mysterious anamorphic object on the canvas at an extremely slanting angle, the angle of the exaggerated point of view adopted by the painter.

The impossibility of identification of an object implied by the anamorphose is a disorder. Yet this sort of disorder has nothing to do with that of projected pigments on a canvas or random crystals on a marble surface. This disorder is introduced into order, as it were, by order itself: anamorphic perspective is but an exaggeration, an apex or climax, of classical perspective. To use an existentialist term, it is nothing but a limit situation (*Grenzsituation*) of perspective.

The proximity vision of a great masterpiece (or, indeed, of any picture) by an eye that gets too close to the canvas is necessarily distorting: the shapes become elongated to the point of reaching a state of anorexy; they lose their identity and become linear, while others which were previously rectilinear become rounded and doughlike. That is what happens to all the objects and characters represented in Holbein's *Ambassadors* (see fig. 3 in the next chapter) when one looks at it from an extremely slanting angle—to all the objects, that is, but one. In the lower portion of the picture, normally misshapen and unrecognizable, a clearly delineated, perfectly recognizable shape emerges: a human skull. By an observer standing at his assigned point of view in front of the painting and thus compelled to look at it orthogonally, it is perceived as a sort of oval blob resembling a loaf of bread. By moving from this assigned point of view to a slanting position, the observer makes the grinning death head appear at the bottom of the canvas.

The *Ambassadors* thus may be designated as belonging to the Vanitas genre, which speaks of the omnipresence of death in the midst of life and is supposed to exhort people to pray and be converted. Yet simultaneously it is a signature, the rebuslike signature of the painter, since in German a death head is sometimes said to be a "hollow bone," *ein hohl(es) Bein*.[4] On a more philosophical level, the interjection of the skull into the normality of the representation may mean that the truth of the art work is the death it contains or which clings to it by essence, making dead what was alive. The skull may also mean that the truth of representation is discovered precisely at the point when representation dies; it is exactly at the moment when representation disappears that one perceives the skull. Or perhaps seeing a picture qua representation necessarily means the obliterating of the death idea that inheres in it as its very ground.

However that may be, the reconstruction process by which the form is perceived implies that a process of deconstruction precedes it. This deconstruction deforms the identifiable representation in which the anamorphic object is hidden. Conversely, seeing the hidden shapes necessarily means the distortion and deconstruction of the containing landscape or figure. Seeing an anamorphic object means hurling the containing surrounding objects and shapes into randomness and disorder. The order and ordering implied by all ocular focusing implies the deconstruction of the background over and against which the object to be focused upon is placed. This type of picture implies a necessary seesawing between order and disorder.

The second exception to the aesthetic tenet that equates beauty to absolute order and imposes distance—the distance of the perspective point of view—as an absolute condition for the apperception of the visual work of art is the *non finito* technique. This product of the Renaissance implies that the artist intentionally leaves the work unfinished. The accidentally incomplete work, the mutilated beautiful fragment or ruin, is not what is meant here.[5]

The expression *non finito* means primarily the foregrounding of matter as coarse *hylē*, or material, over and against the purity and order of form. It is tantamount to a foregrounding of disorder over order, or randomness and noise over organization. Thus the brute matter of which the art object is made is presented overtly to the regard of the observer instead of being hidden underneath a polished surface that gives the illusion of absolute order.

The intentional character of the unfinished in the work of one great artist, Michelangelo, has often been discussed by art historians.[6] There is no need, therefore, to expatiate upon his passion for the uncompleted. Art historians usually attribute it to hidden Neoplatonic tendencies: the artist has to show that he is capable of finding the *concetto* concealed within brute matter.[7] In terms of the dichotomy under the aegis of which this book is placed, this means that the artist, the sculptor, has to rely on his haptic vision, on his sense of touch, rather than on mere optical scanning. We have seen, indeed, in previous chapters that some artists go so far as to flay the human body in order to reveal its mechanism.

Critics, however, have not put forward another sort of hypothesis: the possibility that Michelangelo was acutely aware of the seesaw game between *hylē* and *morphē* that characterizes artistic creation. It is quite possible that one aim of this sculptor—perhaps his essential aim, especially during his late, mannerist years—was the conscious introduction of randomness and noise into classical order.

Concerning this fundamental game of substitution that is always being played between matter and form, one cannot help feeling the irony inherent in the dialectic development of art trends, for it was in the century of abstraction and nonrepresentation that the very avant-garde game between matter and form came to an end. In nonrepresentational art the concept of the unfinished means nothing. It is the artist who decides when the work is finished and only according to the criterion of his or her own "interior necessity," to use a term of Kandinsky's. There is no longer any ideal (or ideological) criterion to measure the extent of completeness. Thus came to an end the dichotomy finished/unfinished, so important as a dynamic principle from the time of Michelangelo to that of Matisse. In nonfigurative art it is the decision—or rather the declaration—of the artist that makes the work "finished."

That raises the question again of the relation between speech act and painting. The nonrepresentational artist does not so much practice the art of the pictorial act—which was all-important in the case of the quattrocento artist, as we saw in chapter II—as the art of an actual speech act: hanging one's picture on the wall of one's studio is tantamount to a declaration of completion.

Verbal Proximity

Everything seems to be quite different in the so-called temporal arts—literature, music, cinema. The notion of unfinished as disorder rests on a conception that sees the work of art as an organic development. This is basically the Aristotelian idea of an art work having its beginning, middle, and end. From the outset, indeed, the work of art had a "just proportion," a "balanced form." In this Aristotelian perspective, to produce unfinished works means that one cuts short the organic development. That is the case with the modern avant-garde currents represented by Joyce, Proust, Stein, and others. All these writers foreground the arbitrariness of their decision to end a work and proclaim that this decision stems from a feeling of interior necessity and not from an organic flow. I see in this a transfer from a speech act attitude which came to be born, first, in the realm of the visual arts.

Yet how does one show the *hylē* of the verbal art work? Is there a brute material when it comes to analyzing the verbal work of art? The verbal work of art is made with language, with the divine logos; can one speak of the "matter" of language? Yuri Lotman, the Balt semiotician, speaks of literature in terms of a "secondary modeling system." And indeed, it seems to be the case that the only way of showing bruteness and matter when one deals

with words is the palimpsest form: show the words of the first system behind the secondary modeling system. In other words, matter, *hylē*, can be
shown as collage: pasting newspaper clippings within the literary text, a
technique used by Dos Passos, or pasting together bits of conversation heard
on the street, as in the poem conversations of Apollinaire. It can also be
shown whenever the creative process is foregrounded and becomes visible.
A poem or a novel which overtly shows how it was made shows *hylē* in the
literary sense of the word. It introduces "noise" into the art work in the
shape of the seesaw game between two systems.

Here one must note the forerunner character of the visual work of art. The
unfinished art object might also have been defined in terms of the seesaw
game between noise and organization. Until now, I have not defined this
term *noise*, which stems from information theory and means the diminishing
of information or the lack of it. If I did not do so it was because it seemed to
me that this notion of noise fits better the modern techniques. Michelangelo
obviously did not think in terms of noise when he foregrounded the brute
matter aspect in his sculptures but rather in terms of disorder.

Noise, however, seems to apply very well to the cubist technique of
papiers collés. *Papiers collés* are genuine noises, bits of odds and ends, newspaper clippings, found in dustbins or wastepaper baskets and cut out more
or less at random in order to be pasted on canvas as heterogeneous elements,
not painted onto it. In collages, on the contrary, the noise aspect is obliter-
ated. When one looks at Max Ernst's *La femme 100 têtes* or *Une semaine de
bonté* one sees only a homogeneous whole in which randomness is barely
perceptible: the procedure implies the very precise cutting out of figures and
their transposition from one set of illustrations to another into which they
are integrated. In the *papiers* by Picasso, Braque, and Gris, it is the heterogeneous that is foregrounded. The newspaper, of course, is not material in the
same sense as the block of marble. It consists of verbal matter that has
already been worked upon.[8] Disorder is produced essentially by the change
of context; it stems from the juxaposition of heterogeneous contexts and not
from the *hylē/morphē* game.

It is probable that the introduction of verbal matter as a sort of shapeless
hylē (similar to the much later *papiers collés*) was a creation of Laurence
Sterne in *Tristram Shandy*. Two examples will suffice: the famous passage in
which the corporal "gives a flourish with his stick thus   ,"[9] and the
passage in which an injunction spoken by a person entering the room where
the writer is engaged in the process of writing is literally pasted into his
book:

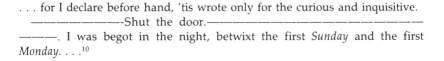

. . . for I declare before hand, 'tis wrote only for the curious and inquisitive.
————————-Shut the door.————————————————
————. I was begot in the night, betwixt the first *Sunday* and the first
Monday. . . .[10]

This noise of the door opening or closing is heard graphically in the work of many later prose writers, from Stendhal, in his numerous sketches of the rooms and houses where he lived and worked, to Proust and beyond.[11] Samuel Beckett recounted how James Joyce accepted the inclusion of interjections pronounced by passing visitors into the manuscript of his "Work in Progress," which Beckett was then typing for Joyce. Inclusions of this sort are extremely numerous in the work of Arno Schmidt, the modern German writer.

As for the anamorphoses found in the visual arts, can one find verbal equivalents for them? It is indeed difficult to speak of an anamorphic effect produced by the proximity of the eye to the text, or even to use the metaphor of the "slanting reading" of a text. The extraction of concealed layers of texts or metaphors may be compared, however, to the extraction of form from the formlessness of the lumpy anamorphic shapes on a canvas.

The passage in *Finnegans Wake* where the defecation of Shem, a scatological writer, is hidden in the labyrinth of a Latin text[12] may, for example, be compared to the anamorphose of Erhard Shön, in which a giant hidden in the landscape may be seen defecating on a shore through the slanting, oblique regard demanded of the anamorphic observer (fig. XI.1). Similarly, the geographic or topographic words on the very first page of *Finnegans Wake* are fragments of hidden sexual anatomies.

The verbal/visual analogy is also true in respect to the seesaw between shape and shapelessness, whether one reads the text or looks at the pictures. *Finnegans Wake* "landscapes" and "cityscapes" lose their topographic character when one sees them as sexual parts, just as Holbein's ambassadors become elongated, shapeless (anamorphic) forms when one perceives the skull hidden in the picture.

Impressionism and Beyond

Impressionism in painting was essentially the rejection of the notion of outline. Things do not have outlines for "real" vision, the impressionists said; they are mere conglomerates of haptic spots of color juxtaposed in space. Thus at one stroke the impressionists did away with the linear, the

XI.1 *Was siehst Du?* Anamorphic landscape by Erhard Schön.
By permission of the Albertina Museum, Vienna.

optical. The world was only a compound of color stains! Lines were eliminated! No wonder the reaction of the art world was so violent—almost as violent as the reaction of the Bolshevik "line" toers to the "impressionistic" Kerenski (see chap. V).

Just like Renaissance perspective, however, impressionism imposes a point of vision on the spectator. If one stands too close, the canvas seems to be merely a chaos of color without identifiable shapes; it takes a certain amount of distance to see the general subject. Yet pleasure at viewing an impressionist masterpiece is not pleasure at the subject but pleasure at seeing how chaos (the chaos of the color dots) becomes order when one discovers the subject which they constitute, in the strict sense of this term, and which, as it were, emerges slowly under one's gaze.

Were there attempts to transpose the doctrine of this absence of line, of this hegemony of haptic vision, to the literary sphere? Certainly symbolism, in its beginnings, seems to have had something in common with the impressionist attitude. Verlaine, in his *Art poétique,* advocated the rejection of the garishness of pure colors in favor of "the gray nuance" and a fundamental imprecision in descriptions of landscapes and characters.

In the sphere of literary theory, the phenomenological doctrine of Roman Ingarden seems to be the closest equivalent to impressionism. What I have in mind is his concept of "indetermination." According to Ingarden, the literary work of art is composed of an infinite number of *Unbestimmtheitstellen* ("indetermination spots").[13] Ingarden explained that when an author replaces the expression "a man," for instance in the sentence "a man appeared on the threshold," by the phrase "an experienced old man," he only does away with a very limited number of indetermination spots; "there remains an infinity of such spots to be suppressed, each of them necessitating an infinity of determinations." Thus the literary text is constituted of spots of determination separated from one another by so many gaps, which the reader must fill mentally if he is to make head or tail of the poem or narrative he is reading. As in the case of visual impressionism, seeing the text from too close a distance would bring out the gaps. Conversely, too great a distance would put the text out of focus, so that nothing in it except a global subject and structure would be perceptible.

Ingarden was well read in art history, and his books reveal his knowledge. It would be interesting to know to what extent his literary theory owes a debt to art historical concepts. I would like to claim, indeed, that his ideas stem at least as much from the haptical doctrine of impressionism as from the phenomenology of Husserl. Very frequently, for instance, he uses the terms (literary) *perspective* and *perspective change.* If he does not actually use the term *anamorphose,* a cognate *terminum tecnicus* appears under his pen in *The Literary Work of Art.* The phrase *die Verkürzungen des Textes* (from the Italian *gli scorti*) refers to the fact that a literary text necessarily exaggerates the perspective of certain depicted objects. Here too a search for the proper distance and the proper focal point is indispensable for the reader.

Certainly there is no doubt that for Ingarden the mere surface of the literary text is a sort of chaos, the equivalent of an impressionist or pointillist disorder, a disorder to which a proper focus and a proper distance must be applied if one is to discern the truth in it. This search for the adequate point of view was tantamount to what Ingarden understood as the concretization of a text.

The search for the proper focus was succeeded in the late 1950s by another type of game: noise itself became the subject of the poem, of the text. This is the case in almost all so-called concrete poetry. I will illustrate this ever-growing consciousness in poets that the actual theme of the literary art work is indeed the dialectic between order and disorder through a series of four poems.

The first is Max Bense's "Random 11.4.59. nachmittags (afternoon)," whose title speaks for itself.[14]

Random 11. 4. 59. nachmittags

verlassen verdeckter Topos wo der Wind den Laut Licht den
Blick abträgt oder vermutet grün Transfer unten Palaver der
drei Männer matter Ton, geschickt verschlossene Tür grauer
Mauer um totes Haus in Bilignin kleiner Ort auf keiner Karte
oberhalb Belley noch in Ain und im Regen, verschlossene
Frauen verschlossen verbleibt was alt ist und welches Da-
sein nützt noch dem Sein wenn dein kleiner Hund dich nicht
kennt so bricht endlich für hinziehn flußwärts das was was

Similarly, Timm Ulrich's "Ordnung (Order)" is clear enough.[15]

```
ordnung     ordnung
ordnung     ordnung
ordnung     ordnung
ordnung     ordnung
ordnung     ordnung
ordnung  unordn    g
ordnung     ordnung
ordnung     ordnung
ordnung     ordnung
ordnung     ordnung
ordnung     ordnung
```

Cavan McCarthy's "rendering the legible illegible," from *Poem for Deborah*, defined the global aim of this movement in a very lapidary manner.[16]

rendering the legible illegible
rendering the il**legible**
rend̶e̶t̶l̶e̶g̶i̶b̶t̶h̶e̶
r̶e̶̶h̶d̶g̶r̶b̶t̶g̶

And in "noises" by Helmut Heissenbüttel the introduction of noises that resemble those made by a transmission in Morse code helped define this little "misuk" (Brecht's word for *Musik*) of concrete poetry.[17]

ismus **ta ti** istisch **ti ta ti ta to ti ti to** istisch
ta ta to ta istisch **ti** ismus **ti ti to ti** istisch
ta ta ismus **to to ti** ismus **ti to** istisch **ta ti**
ta istisch ismus **to to ta to ti ta to ta ta**
to ismus **ta** ismus **ti to to ta ta to** istisch **ti**
ta to ismus **ta** ismus istisch **ti** istisch **ta ta to**
istisch **ti ta ti ti ta to ti ti ti to ta** ismus **to**
to istisch **ti ti to ti to ti ta ta ti to ta ti**
ti istisch **ti** ismus **ti ta to** istisch **to ta** istisch
to to to ti ta to to ta ti istisch **ta to** ismus
ti ismus **to** istisch ismus **ta** istisch **ti ti to to**
ismus **ta ti ti ta** istisch **ti** istisch **ta** ismus **ta**
to ta to ta to to ta to ismus **to to** ismus
to ta ti ta istisch **ti ta ta ti ta** istisch ismus
to ta istisch **to to ta ti to to** ismus **ti to ti**
ismus **ti ti ti** ismus **ta** ismus **ti ta** istisch

The poem by Bense is not more explicit than the others concerning the hypostasis of the game order/disorder, yet I consider it an index for the whole movement. Bense not only is a foremost German semiotician and editor of *Semiosis*, the journal published by Stuttgart University; he is also a theorist of entropy as a principle capable of contributing to the creation of artistic forms.[18] I believe that beyond the entropy principle, beyond this disorder principle within the essential order of "reasonable aesthetics," concrete poetry is the result of a substitution that took place in a historical context. Indeed, it was at the very moment when the game *hylē/morphē*, matter/form, which had dominated the art scene for so long, had become impossible that concrete poetry appeared. When this game became impossible because of the hegemony of nonrepresentational aesthetic, it was to a large extent this movement that picked up the fallen relay and introduced a new aesthetic. It asked the reader to start reading order as disorder and disorder as order. That, perhaps, corresponded to the real intention of the action painters; over and beyond their gesticulation and their dance, didn't they ask us, these gesticulating artists, to read a meaning into their labyrinth of optic lines?

XII

OCULOCENTRISM AND
ITS DISCONTENTS

This chapter, the last in the book, is also the one which deals with the death of sight and with the discovery that death is at the very core and center of sight. Death is, dialectically, always present as a concealed watermark in those periods which represent a climactic exaltation of the sense of sight. It is indeed the irony of dialectical evolution—or rather of the revolutionary stage within evolution—that things taken for granted eventually turn against themselves and negate their own existence or, conversely, being nonexistent at first glance, eventually assert their invisible presence.

What greater irony than a treatise on color written by a blind man? Such was the case in the sixteenth century when the blind Lomazzo wrote his *Idea of the Temple of Painting*. At specific points in our human history the eye has turned against itself, turned against its own "oculocentrism" and murdered sight.[1]

One such point of reversal corresponded with the Renaissance, with the triumph of perspective. Testifying to this destruction of sight by sight in the midst of the exaltation of sight is a scene in a picture by Mantegna, *Archers Shooting at Saint Christopher*. Placed in an upper corner, the scene shows how a spectator to Christopher's martyrdom is inadvertently blinded by an arrow sent by one of the archers. One critic, Michael Kubovy, has commented on the "arrow-like" quality of perspective as it was perceived by Renaissance man. Indeed, this very fragment of the Mantegna picture was used on the cover of the paperback edition of Kubovy's book. As Kubovy writes, "There is a frightening detail . . . that shows a man who has just been shot with an arrow. I see the arrow in the eye as a metaphor for the art of perspective." Kubovy then introduces a number of examples from the writings of Alberti and Filarete showing that the art of marksmanship with bow and arrow was seen as the model of perspective construction. Arrows, however, were simultaneously "blinding" for the "innocent eye."[2]

Another such dialectical turning point, it seems to me, came in the years following the First World War, the age of expressionism and abstraction. Oculocentrism prevailed in those years, just as it did in the Renaissance. The term *oculocentrism* refers to the hegemony of the sense of sight over the other senses. It was coined by a modern historian of philosophy, Martin Jay, who asserts that our postmodern society is essentially oculocentrist—for better and for worse. Jay has pronounced this statement in conferences and written it in articles, in a context of postmodernism and deconstructionist agitation.[3] Indeed, Jay's posture to a certain extent parallels Jacques Derrida's claim that modern or postmodern society is essentially "logocentrist," privileging speech above all other things. For Jay, perhaps more perceptive than Derrida, in postmodern society it is the sense of sight and the visual that are overduly privileged.

In the case of logocentrism—that is, in the case of the modern confrontation with texts and with oral language defied by language embodied in texts—remedies meant to ensure the victory of visual language have been devised which are many and varied. From the decision to defer permanently the search for meaning and the fixation of meaning to the ultimate deconstructionist techniques which foreground all "flaws" in discourse, a variety of procedures are at hand which permit the neutralization of the hegemonic language of logocentrism.

Yet, is it not so with oculocentrist hegemony? In the visual field, did deconstruction wait until the appearance of the Derridian treatises to become the order of the day? It is a fact that the hegemony of the eye was glorified and vilified simultaneously by "eye artists" (if one may indulge in this Kafkaesque neologism, *Augenkünstler*).

The revolt against the enslavement of the eye by its own all-devouring visuality—its visual appetite—and against the manipulators of this appetite has long taken place. As was to be expected, the organizers of the revolt were the manipulators of the eye themselves, the visual artists and the cinema directors who lived by the eye. I am referring here to the revolt, implicit and explicit, which took place during the 1920s, to movements such as dada and surrealism and to such people as Salvador Dali and Luis Buñuel, the makers of *Un Chien Andalou;* their dada and postdada contemporaries in France; and their fellow artists in revolutionary Russia, the constructivists. In the literary sphere, the main protagonist of the revolt was Georges Bataille, with his "Histoire de l'oeil"—a rather ambiguous title which may mean either "a story about an eye" or "the history of the eye." As a matter of fact, the story told by Bataille is really that of "the end of the eye," its self-castration.

If one considers the movements just mentioned, one cannot fail to observe that all those modern artists, those skillful manipulators of our regard, while ostensibly celebrating the primacy of gaze, were also talking about the unbearable character of true seeing, about the trauma of sight. The modernist eye is no longer enlisted into the service of an appeal function or a conative function; it no longer seeks our regard, as did the figure of the demonstrator, or expositor, which I analyzed in chapter II. The fetishized presence of the eye signals, paradoxically, the end of vision.

XII.1 Poster for Dziga Vertov's *Kino Glaz*.
By permission of the Johns Hopkins University
Press, Baltimore.

The image in *Un Chien Andalou* of the slicing of the eye of a young woman
with a razor blade was not born in a vacuum. Modern publicity, constructivist posters, even a film by Buñuel's great precursor Dziga Vertov, *The Man
with a Camera,* all show the human eye as an autonomous organ, almost as
detached, or rather severed, from the human head of which it is supposed to
be an organic part. The poster for Vertov's *Kino Glaz* shows this severing of
the eye, which has now become an object of observation for the gaze of the
observer, as if it were a sort of planet or satellite hovering in the sky (fig.
XII.1).[4] The magazine *Novy Lef* similarly showed on its cover another autonomous eye.[5]

Are these premonitory statements that we see here, or merely an exaltation of the sense of sight? Or are they the expression of a semiconscious fear?
In actual historical fact, the eye of the artist was about to be castrated by
what Georg Lukács called "vulgar Marxism," the Stalinist variety. And all
avant-garde artists in the Soviet Union must have felt at the time that they
were being watched by the all-seeing party and its police. This is really what
comes to the fore in this omnipresence of the severed and fetishized eye.

Yet in France, a country where there was no omnipresent party dictator-
ship, the eye also appears fragmented and sliced out of real organic existence. A poster from the 1920s shows the severed eyeball horribly staring at
us (fig. XII.2).[6] And the surrealist Magritte in 1932 painted a sliced eye pic-

XII.2 *Tabu*, a French poster of 1921.
Collection, Museum of Modern Art, New York;
by permission.

ture entitled *The Object (The Eye).*[7] What is perhaps Magritte's most famous painting, *The False Mirror* at the Museum of Modern Art in New York, in a way also represents a severed eyeball.[8]

Magritte's work is perhaps less a proclamation of the objective character of vision than a debunking of this objectivity: the eye is shown as reified, frozen on a disk. But Magritte leaves open a third possibility: the debunking may concern the essential voyeurism of the human eye. And one never knows whether Magritte's female eye is watching us through a round hole in a black partition or whether it is truly an object, a representation of a human eye on a piece of canvas. However that may be, Magritte's picture is reminiscent of an eye that was placed as an insert at intervals in Fernand Léger's film *Ballets Mécaniques*. It is also reminiscent of an eye slice construction at about the same time by the American surrealist Man Ray, a photograph of an eye disk pasted on the rhythmical arm of a metronome. The title of this construction too is oxymoronic: *Indestructible Object* evokes both the eternal subjectivity of the human eye and its fateful reification.

Even the German expressionist cinema showed this terrible autonomy of the eye. In the classic *Überfall* by Ernö Metzner, it seems to flow out of its socket, as though it were a liquid substance.[9] In the 1923 film *Die Strasse* by Karl Grune, the street itself plays a role and enters directly into the action. At one point the protagonist, solicited by a prostitute, finds himself being stared at by a gigantic pair of eyes: a publicity device for an optometrist's shop. For the hero, these eyes become the gaze of diabolical forces which seem to surround him.

Had F. Scott Fitzgerald seen this film when he wrote *The Great Gatsby*? His novel contains a passage strongly reminiscent of *Die Strasse:*

> About half way between West Egg and New York the motor road hastily joins the railroad and runs beside it for a quarter of a mile, so as to break away from a certain area of land. This is a valley of ashes—a fantastic farm where ashes grow like wheat into ridges and hills and grotesque gardens; where ashes take the forms of houses and chimneys and rising smoke, and finally, with a tran-scendent effort, of ash-gray men who move dimly and already crumbling through the powdery air. . . . But above the gray land and the spasms of bleak dust which drift suddenly over it, you perceive, after a moment, the eyes of Doctor T. J. Eckleburg. The eyes of Doctor T. J. Eckleburg are blue and gigan-tic—their retinas are one yard high. They look out of no face, but, instead, from a pair of enormous yellow spectacles which pass over a non-existent nose. Evidently, some wild wag of an oculist set them down there to fatten his practice in the borough of Queens and then sank down himself into eternal blindness. . . . But his eyes, dimmed a little by the many paintless days, under sun and rain, brood on over the solemn dumping ground.[10]

In this passage, too, seeing and blindness (what is more, "eternal" blindness) are equated and constitute a sort of antithetical couple, an oxymoron. But wasn't the whole surrealist scene oxymoronic in its conception of the eye as glorification of sight and fear of seeing at one and the same time?

The theme of the empty eyes, the empty Eckleburg spectacles, recurred in the dark hours of the Second World War in the work of the German painter Max Beckmann, who was living in exile in Holland. His picture *Genius* is an advertisement for a pair of huge, opaque eyeglasses. Through them one sees nothing. Beckmann must have been debunking the romantic idea of genius, of his own genius, at a time when the word was empty and meaningless, when all that counted was physical courage and brutal force in the final onslaught against Nazi Germany.[11] Germany was a "valley of ashes" one did not want to see, and Beckmann's glasses were the sign of an imposed blindness, of a proud German artist's refusal to see the horror.

The cruelest statement on the fundamental impotency of the eye undoubt-edly was pronounced by the protosurrealist Bataille in his poem "L'anus solaire": "The human eye is unable to look at the sun, at an act of copula-tion, at a cadaver, at total obscurity. . . ."[12] One of the erotic games played by the narrator of Bataille's "Histoire de l'oeil" and his mistress, Simone, concerns the equivalence of egg and eye.

> When I asked what suggested to her the word *urinate*, she answered *sever*, sever the eye with a razor, or something red, the sun. How about *egg*? A calf's eye, because of the color [of veal] and also because the white of the egg is the same substance as the white of the eye. She wanted me to promise that . . . we would shatter eggs with revolver shots, high in the air in the sun. . . . She

played on words, gaily, and would now use the expression *break an eye*, now *break an egg*, and indulged in unbearable reflections on the subject.[13]

The analogy between the eye and the sexual organs—in this case, perhaps, the male organs more than the female—becomes even more apparent in the subsequent chapter, when Simone is invited to attend a bullfight. After the fight and the traditional castration of the bull, she demands to be given the animal's testicles.

> At the spot where Simone was to be seated, in the sun, there was a white plate on which rested two testicles which had been skinned. They were glands shaped like an egg, mother-of-pearl white, barely pink as an eye is pink: they had just been taken from the first bull. . . .[14]

Later the horrified and "fascinated" spectators witness the death of the torero under the horn thrusts of the bull: "a blow of the horn gored the right eye and the whole head. . . . Men rushed into the arena and carried on their arms the body of Granero whose right eye was dangling out of its socket."[15]

The genital organ of woman also is "like an eye." Simone plays substitution games and introduces eggs into her vulva. The story ends when the narrator discovers one day that the substitute eye is a real one, that of a girl who had died or been murdered: "I could see, very clearly, the pale blue eye of Simone inserted in the hairy vagina of Simone. It looked at me and was shedding urine tears."[16]

I have not been able to discover whether Dali and Buñuel knew Bataille's story and had been inspired by it before they filmed *Un Chien Andalou* or whether Bataille, on the contrary, was moved to write his tale after seeing the film. The chronological ordering of Bataille's complete works in French gives the impression that his tale preceded the shooting of the film by a few months or years. Yet the masterpiece of Dali and Buñuel is mentioned at length in a pseudo-encyclopedic article entitled "Eye," which Bataille wrote in 1929. In it Bataille mentions an irresistible association between *eye* and *blade* provoked by the view of a human pupil. It was such an association, he writes, that must have compelled "two young Catalans" to make their "extraordinary" film, "so totally different from the banal avant-garde productions of the period."[17]

Another source for the extraordinary scene in *Un Chien Andalou*—and perhaps also for Bataille's story—is Federico García Lorca's short story "Santa Lucia and San Lazaro."[18] Santa Lucia was the Christian saint who tore out her eyes to free herself from worldly temptation, from temptations of the flesh. The militant atheists Lorca and Buñuel knew the terrible visual temptations of big city life and also what one might call the temptation of visual castration. Yet they had no use for the Christian saint who embodied this self-castration. For Lorca, Santa Lucia became a sort of modernist machine or robot: "Her enormous body was made of compressed lead." Lorca metamorphosed this Christian goddess of self-blinding into a symbol of the terrible artificial sight apparatus of the modern city:

> All the streets were full of optical shops. From the doorways gazed large megatheric eyes—terrible eyes looking out of an almond-shaped orbit. . . . Spectacles and smoked glasses sought the immense lopped-off hand of the glove shop, a poem in the air that rang bled and bubbled like the head of John the Baptist.[19]

All that remains of the hero's "saintly" experience at the end of the story is a pair of goggles, which "raised to a maximum their concrete construction of a superior reality."[20] Concrete reality has become a simulacrum of vision!

Epater—or at least *provoquer*—*le bourgeois* certainly was one aim of Bataille and his two surrealist friends. This provocation, however, was done not through language, as had been the case with romanticism, but through the image of the castrated eye, textual or cinematographic. The eye of the bourgeois, Bataille keeps saying, is castrated. It is therefore necessary to represent the castrating process. Only the brutal truth of visual violence, Bataille writes, can "uncastrate": "One cannot remain blind to the fact that horror becomes a process of fascination, and also that it is the only power that is violent enough to explode stifling repression."[21]

One must force oneself to look at the "unbearable": the sun, copulating couples, dead bodies, obscurity, and, of course, castration itself, in the form of the sliced eye. This forcible training of one's regard upon the unbearable is not without danger; at the end of his "Eye" article, Bataille tells us that Buñuel was sick for a whole week after shooting the eye and razor scene. In the best of cases, this prolonged nausea is the price one must pay for defying visual repression. And yet visual violence is a veritable duty that one must perform in order to free humankind. The beginning of freedom, Bataille—and Buñuel—might write, begins with a rape, a rape of the eye.

It must be noted that a real case of violent blinding occurred during these surrealist years. In the early 1930s Victor Brauner, a painter who had represented himself on canvas several times as a Cyclops, was gored in one eye by a colleague during a drinking bout in a surrealist hangout. The Spanish painter Dominguez did it with a single blow of the glass out of which he was drinking. Certainly it was not an act of provocation directed against the bourgeoisie. It was more likely an action that expressed the prevailing malaise of the artists at their own oculocentrism. Dominguez's action was as paradigmatic for his time as Mantegna's arrow in the eye of his spectator was for the Renaissance. At the same time it reveals an obsession with the eye as a quasi sexual organ or substitute for sex, a view that, as we shall see shortly, was the foundation for Lacan's neo-Freudian theories.

It is somewhat surprising to observe that the very process that was so liberating for Bataille, Dali, and Buñuel was seen, half a century later, as a process of repression. I am referring to the view presented in *A Clockwork Orange*, both the novel by Anthony Burgess and its filmed version by Stanley Kubrick. The young hoodlum Alex is submitted to a "visual cure." Strapped into a chair, his eyelids pinned up by clamps which prevent them from covering the pupils so that the eyeballs are permanently exposed to visual stimuli, he is forced to watch violent and lurid movies in which scenes of rape and murder are presented in great detail. Such visual violence triggers nausea in him just as it did in the young Buñuel, but with the difference that instead of liberating Alex's aggressive and sexual impulses it causes him to permanently repress them.

Both Burgess and Kubrick attribute extremes of power to the film medium. Like the surrealists, like Bataille, they are awed by the power of the image, by the power it seems to wield—through the eye—over the human psyche. But the Burgess novel and the Kubrick film clearly are situated in a context different from that of the Bataille story and the Buñuel film: the eye is manipulated by social forces within the framework of a social practice of a certain kind. *A Clockwork Orange* ends with a clear allusion to television manipulation as a group of journalists are ushered in together with their cameramen to record the "new and beautiful friendship" between the justice minister and his supposed victim, Alex. In such a context the television camera—just like the movie camera in front of which Alex is strapped—is presented as an instrument for lying and manipulating the masses, not for liberating the individual.

Burgess, incidentally, also wrote his own story of the eye. Entitled "Evil Eye," it may be seen as a sort of delayed conclusion to the story of violent Alex and his artificially lashed hoodlum eye. "I have seen," Burgess writes, "Roman prostitutes make the apotropaic horn-gesture in the presence of a priest. This is not . . . because a priest is a monster—a mixture of skirted woman and celibate man—but because, having given up the joys of copulation, priests have received the *mallochial* gift in compensation." The *malocchio* is of course the evil eye. "It is noteworthy," Burgess adds, "that the response to the *malocchio* is a phallic gesture or symbol—the power of male generation against female destruction."[22]

Burgess here formulates precisely what was only implicit in Bataille's story: that there is a sort of inverse proportionality between sex as phallus and sex as vulva. In other words, vision in woman is a phallic thrust, which can only be countered by an opposite thrust of a real phallus equivalent, the "horn-gesture" with the thumb and index finger of the hand. In chapter II we saw that the gesture of demonstration is an act of cooperation between the finger and the eye. Below this intellectual and spiritual level, in the dark fonts of the collective psyche, may be found a deeper layer in which the "female" eye and the "male" index finger are implacable enemies.

When Jacques Lacan, with his cultural roots in surrealism, coined the phrase "scopic function" (sometimes translated "scopotopic pulsion"), it was merely a conceptual crystallization, a name giving, for something that existed already in Bataille's and Buñuel's works and in surrealism in general.[23] Nonetheless, the equivalence between the act of visual apperception, the regard, and some sort of sexual act was for the first time given an officially psychoanalytic stamp by the leader of the self-styled *école freudienne* in Paris.

In a negative way, of course, sex and the eye had always been associated. From the very beginning of his psychoanalytic writings, Freud saw the self-blinding of Oedipus as an act of self-castration. Yet Freud never wrote of sight or vision as a positive act, as an act of creation or even procreation, let alone of the human constitution. Though Freud probably did not know it, incest and visuality are associated in classical Hebrew. The usual phrase designating the act of incest is *gilui arayot*, "the uncovering of the sexual parts" of the parent. This phrase is used in the biblical episode of Noah's drunkenness, when his sons see his genitals. In Sophocles' *Oedipus*, self-castration is signified by the putting out of one's own eyes, but in the Bible the beginning of incest is described in terms of a visual act.

Thus it fell to Lacan, not Freud, to formulate the equation eye = sex, with apperception seen in terms of a thrust or drive of the eye toward a sexual object. Sex comes to the fore not only in acts of extreme visual repression such as self-blinding but also in ordinary vision. As a matter of fact, it may be claimed that during a lifetime of teaching and publishing Lacan wrote chiefly about this scopic pulsion, even when it remained unnamed in his writings. Indeed, isn't the human person—according to Lacan's theories—actually constituted by the young child through the visual apperception of his body in a mirror?

This visual activity is not merely apperceptual; it is creative or constitutive of what is called the self. It is through the eye that one enters the realm of what Lacan calls "the Imaginary" as opposed to "the Symbolic," which is more the realm of language (although it may also be located at a deeper level of the apperceptive act). One might say that this act of self-constituting begun in the mirror by the power of the eye continues throughout life. There is no absolute limit between procreation and creating one's own self through an act of vision.

For Lacan, speaking about visuality and the power of images was simultaneously speaking about sex and sexual impulses. Yet for him, too, the power of the eye might in certain cases turn against itself. Moreover, the eye was the subject of social acts of castration. Lacan certainly saw bourgeois culture as an instrument of castration through the eye. As noted earlier in this book, the "letter" which, in Lacan's description of Poe's "Purloined Letter," lay sprawling in the middle of the table—indeed, in the middle of the whole room—like "a gigantic woman body" could not be perceived any longer by the castrated eye. Under the impact of repressive blows, the eye and the sexual desires which reside essentially in the eye were forever blinded, self-castrated.

XII.3 *The Ambassadors* by Holbein the Younger.
Photo National Gallery, London; by permission.

Another of Lacan's paradigms for this self-blinding of human vision, for the death of the eye contained in the very act of apperception, is a specific anamorphose, the one that, as Lacan expresses it, "hovers in the fore-ground" of Holbein's *Ambassadors* at the National Gallery in London (fig. XII.3).[24] Let us hear Lacan himself speak about this "hovering shape" in the lower center of the painting:

> How strange that no one ever thought of evoking the effect of an erection. Imagine a tattooed male member and the shape the drawing would take, once this member had reached its maximum size. What exactly is this elongated shape which looks like a flying object or a diagonally inclined mass? You cannot know it—because you avert your gaze from it in order to escape the fascination of the picture. But if you start leaving the room, and turn around for a last glance, you suddenly capture the mysterious form: it was a death skull. . . . To me this painted skull suggested one of those loaves of bread that Dali, in his youth, used to set on the head of an old hag he chose as slatternly as possible . . . or the "soft watches" of this same painter, of which the mean-

ing is no less phallic than the flying object in the foreground of *The Ambassadors*.

To understand the phenomenon of perception: the subject here is not the one who is active in reflexive consciousness but the one who is active in desire. One believes that what is at stake here is the concept of the geometric point of vision, whereas the [real eye] is another sort of eye: the sort that is hovering in the foreground of *The Ambassadors*. The regard is not the Eye, except under the aspect of this hovering form through which Holbein has brazenly dared to show me my own soft watch.[25]

The anamorphic shape, as long as it is not recreated, reconstituted, is an erection; and yet, in order to be recreated and identified, the object must undergo a detumescence, a deflation. Reconstituted, it becomes a death's head, a skull. Eros must be followed by Thanatos. The anamorphic skull makes manifest, visible, the idea of the gaze as a pulsion, a scopic pulsion. The eye too is an extension of the phallus. Simultaneously, Lacan extends the notion of seeing as erection/deflation to the total phenomenon of vision, especially artistic or aesthetic vision. Indeed, the act of seeing according to the code of classical—that is, Italian—perspective, proceeding as it does from the so-called point of vision to the vanishing point in which all the perspective lines converge, can also be described as erection/deflation. The perspective lines cause us to erect our gaze toward the vanishing point, but then observation vanishes, becomes nil, passes into death, as Kleist might have said. The anamorphose is a point of convergence between the image and its death or negation, the coinciding of a picture of Eros with its truth, the image of Thanatos, in one and the same shape. Seeing is both an erotic sexual pulsion and a passage into death, its apparent opposite.

The anamorphic skull represents an element of paramount importance for Lacan: a point of convergence. And this convergence is for him the coinciding of the Imaginary, which relates to the constitution of an image as a totality, especially that of one's own body image (as for instance in a mirror), and the Symbolic, which is actually the deconstruction of this image and the revelation of the absolute Other, Death, that is behind language and behind the visual image. Lacan's oculocentrism is a thanatocentrism.[26]

NOTES

I. Touching with the Eye

1. Courbet's letter to Champfleury is reproduced in Alan Bowness, "The Painter's Studio," in *Courbet in Perspective*, ed. Petra Ten-Doesschate Chu (Englewood Cliffs, N.J., 1975), pp. 130–140. See esp. p. 136. See also Benedict Nicolson, *Courbet: The Studio of the Painter* (London, 1973), pp. 13–16.

2. On this hieroglyphic genealogy of emblems, see Claude-Françoise Breugnon, "Signe, figure, langage: Les hiéroglyphes d'Horapollo," in the proceedings of the Tours colloquium *L'emblème à la Renaissance* (Paris, 1982), pp. 29–49.

3. Reproduced in *Emblematik und Drama im Zeitalter des Barocks* (Munich, 1964), fig. 88.

4. See D. A. Alciati, *Emblemata* (Lyons, 1550), p. 22.

5. See, for instance, E. S. Gifford, *The Evil Eye* (New York, 1958); M. S. Thomson, "Evil-eye Charms," *Folklore* 19 (1908); T. Schire, *Hebrew Amulets* (London, 1966); and Frederick Ellworthy, *The Evil Eye* (London, 1895; reprinted New York, 1958).

6. This famous self-portrait is frequently reproduced in works on mannerism. See, for instance, G. R. Hocke, *Die Welt als Labyrinth* (Hamburg, 1966), fig. 1.

7. Georges Bataille, *Oeuvres complètes*, vol. 1 (Paris, 1970), p. 187.

8. Lacan's "scopic function" recurs quite often in the unpublished *cahiers* of his "Séminaire" (not always under that term). See, for example, *Le séminaire, Livre XI: Les quatre concepts fondamentaux de la psychanalyse* (Paris, 1975), esp. "Du regard," pp. 79–107.

9. Later this dichotomy was renamed by another great art historian, Heinrich Wölfflin, who spoke of the linear (*das Linearische*) versus the painterly (*das Malerische*). See his most famous work, *Kunsthistorische Grundbegriff: Das Problem der Stilentwicklung in der neueren Kunst* (Munich, 1921), pp. 20–80.

10. René Descartes, "Discours I," in *La dioptrique* (1902), pp. 85–86.

11. Maurice Merleau-Ponty, *L'oeil et l'esprit* (Paris, 1960), p. 56.

12. George Berkeley, "An Essay toward a New Theory of Vision," in *Works on Vision*, ed. with a commentary by Colin Murray Turbayne (New York and Indianapolis, 1963), pp. 19–102. Originally published in 1710.

13. Ibid., p. 2.

14. One cannot help observing here that this formulation is very close to—or rather prefigures—Roman Jakobson's description of the poetic function as the "projection of the metonymic axis over the metaphor axis."

15. Georg Wilhelm Friedrich Hegel, *Aesthetics: Lectures on the Fine Arts* (Oxford, 1975).

16. A. L. Yarbus, *Rol Dvizhenij Glaz v Protsesse Zrenya* (Institute for the Transmission of Information of the Academy of the Sciences of the USSR/Nauka Press), p. 110, n. 10.

17. The apparatus recording eye movements is described in David Noton and Lawrence Stark, "Eye Movements and Visual Perception," in *Image, Object, Illusion* (San Francisco, 1971), p. 117.

18. Viktor Lowenfeld, *Creative and Mental Growth* (New York, 1952), p. 230. Lowenfeld emigrated to the United States in 1933 because of racial persecutions in his native Germany.

19. See Alois Riegl, *Die Spaetantique Kunstindustrie* (Vienna, 1901; 2d ed., 1927; rpt. 1964).

20. E. Llewellyn Thomas, "Eye Movements in Speed Reading," in R. G. Stauffer, ed., *Speed Reading: Practices and Procedures* (Newark, Del., 1962), pp. 104–114.

II. The Gesture of Demonstration

1. *Ausdruck/Darstellung/Appel.* See Karl Bühler, *Sprachtheorie: über die Darstellungsfunktion der Sprache* (Stuttgart, 1934, 1965).

2. Wolfgang Iser, *Die Appelfunktion des Textes* (Konstanz, 1971).

3. See, in particular, George Kernodle, *From Art to Theater* (Chicago, 1944).

4. J. L. Austin, *How to Do Things with Words* (Cambridge, Mass., 1962).

5. Michel Foucault, *Les mots et les choses* (Paris, 1966), pp. 19–31. Similarly, Louis Marin, in his analysis of a painting by Le Brun—a cartoon for a tapestry—stated that the "reality effect" in seventeenth-century painting was produced through "la dénégation du sujet de l'énonciation." In this type of painting the enunciated image seems to "present itself to the viewer" as though by the agency of its own autonomous action and as though the historical scene were happening under the very gaze of the observer and at the time of his or her observation. See Marin, *A propos d'un carton de Le Brun: Le tableau d'histoire et la dénégation de l'énonciation* (Centre International de Sémiologie et de Linguistique d'Urbino, Document de Travail 41, série F).

6. Giovanni-Battista Alberti, *Della Pittura* (Florence, 1955), p. 123; my translation.

7. Umberto Eco, *A Theory of Semiotics* (Bloomington, Ind., 1978), sec. 3.4.10.

8. Yarbus, *Rol Dvizhenij Glaz v Protsesse Zrenya*; Noton and Stark, "Eye Movements and Visual Perception," in *Image, Object, Illusion*, pp. 113–122.

9. On the concept of metastability, see Claude Gandelman, "The Metastability of Signs/Metastability as a Sign," *Semiotica* 28 (1979): 83–105.

10. Eco, *Theory of Semiotics*, pp. 315–318.

11. On ostention, see Yvo Osolsobe, "On Ostensive Communication," *Studia Semiotyczne* 9 (1972): 65–75.

12. See Pál Kelemen, *El Greco Revisited* (New York, 1961), p. 123.

13. Louis Marin, "Signe et représentation: Philippe de Champaigne et Port-Royal," *Etudes Sémiologiques* (Paris, 1971), pp. 127–159. See also Claude Gandelman, "La déiconisation janséniste de l'art: Pascal, Philippe de Champaigne," *Le regard dans le texte* (Paris, 1986), pp. 95–119.

14. Emile Benvéniste, *Essais de linguistique générale* (Paris, 1966), esp. chap. 20.

15. Bibliothèque Nationale, Paris, Rés. Ye 120 (BN).

16. Laurence Sterne, *The Life and Opinions of Tristram Shandy, Gentleman* (New York, 1959), p. 503.

17. Ibid., p. 56.

18. Quoted in Wayne C. Booth, *Rhetoric of Fiction* (Chicago, 1961), p. 216.

19. Brecht implicitly recognized his debt to the great *philosophe* when he decided to promote the idea of a Diderot Society in Germany.

III. Penetrating Doors

1. See Arnold Van Gennep, *Les rites de passage* (Paris, 1909).

2. See esp. Victor Turner, *The Forest of Symbols: Aspects of Ndembu Ritual* (Ithaca, N.Y., 1958).

3. Among the more recent works on the subject, see Julian Gallego, *El cuadro dentro del cuadro* (Madrid, 1978).

4. Chastel's study is included in his *Fables, formes, figures* (Paris, 1978), pp. 145–154.

5. The catalogue of the French Art Museum Collections attributes the *Babooshes* to Samuel Van Hoogstraten.

6. See the entry "square, semiotic" in A. J. Greimas and J. Courtés, *Semiotics and Language: An Analytical Dictionary*, trans. Larry Crist et al. (Bloomington, Ind., 1982).

7. On the relation between the semiotics of A. J. Greimas and medieval dialectics, see M. Blanché, *Structures intellectuelles* (Paris, 1966), and esp. Alain de Libéra, "La sémiotique d'Aristote," *Structures élémentaires de la signification* (Paris, 1976), pp. 28–49.

8. See, for instance, José Gudiol, *Velasquez* (London, 1974), p. 288.

9. This *Vanitas* is well in keeping with the seventeenth-century moralizing tradition.

10. Bühler's *Ausdruck/Darstellung/Appel* as formulated in his *Sprachstudien*, transposed from language functions to text functions.

11. To Bühler's three functions Jakobson—acknowledging his debt to his German precursor—added the function of contact (the phatic function); the poetic function (expressing the sui generis character of the poetic message); and the metalinguistic function (language which talks about language).

12. Not only Jakobson but Wolfgang Iser too has appropriated this term of Bühler's. See Iser, *Die Appelstruktur des Textes: Unbestimmtheit als Wirkungsbedingung literarischer Prosa* (Munich, 1970).

13. See the entries "euphoria" and "dysphoria" in Greimas and Courtés, *Semiotics and Language*. See also Greimas, *Du sens* (Paris, 1970), pp. 282–283.

14. See, for instance, Vermeer's *Maid and Lady with a Letter* (*The Love Letter*) at the Rijksmuseum, reproduced in *The Complete Paintings of Vermeer* (New York, 1979), pl. XLVII. See also *The Street*, pl. XXVII.

15. Heinrich Wölfflin, *Fundamental Principles of Art History* (New York, 1963), pp. 102–108.

16. H. C. Trumbull, *The Threshold Covenant* (New York, 1896).

17. On the idea of the church as the body of Christ, see, for instance, Leonard Barkan, *Nature's Work of Art* (New Haven, Conn., 1975), pp. 69ff.

18. Turner, *Forest of Symbols*, pp. 93–110.

19. Foucault refers to this looking glass in the introduction to *Les mots et les choses*, p. 15.

20. For Foucault, however, the word *spectacle* seems to be operative: "the painting is a spectacle" performed for the benefit of "another spectacle"—the king and queen and their courtiers.

21. It is also a rebuslike signature: a skull, in German, is a "hollow bone," *ein hohl (es) Bein.*

22. Jean-Paul Sartre, *L'imaginaire* (Paris, 1966), pp. 244–245; my translation.

23. Ibid., p. 246.

24. Thomas Sebeok and Harriet Margolis, "Captain Nemo's Port Hole," *Poetics Today* 3 (no. 1, 1982): 110–139.

25. Gustave Flaubert, *Madame Bovary*, trans. Francis Steegmuller (New York, 1957), p. 14.

26. Ibid., p. 58.

27. Ibid., p. 124.

28. Ibid., p. 136.

29. Ibid., p. 274.

30. Ibid., p. 383.

31. Orson Welles used this story in cartoon form as a sort of preamble to his film version of the Kafka novel.

32. Franz Kafka, *The Trial* (New York, 1970), p. 213.

33. Ibid., p. 215.

34. The same is true, of course, of the prolonged reading of a great painting.

35. That, at least, was the interpretation of a great Kafka scholar, Heinz Politzer, in his *Franz Kafka der Künstler* (Frankfurt am Main, 1965). In German, Kafka uses the expression "der Man vom Land."

IV. Optics in Extremis

1. It is reproduced in Lotte Eisner, *The Haunted Screen: Expressionism in the German Cinema, and the Influence of Max Reinhardt* (London, 1965), p. 255.

2. Many of these figures illustrate the cover of the German paperback edition of Kafka's works published by Fischer. They were reproduced for the first time in Max Brod, *Franz Kafkas Glauben und Lehre* (Winterthur and Munich, 1948).

3. Claude Gandelman, "Kafka as an Expressionist Draftsman," *Neohelicon* 2 (nos. 3–4, 1974), pp. 237–257.

4. A self-portrait in gouache is at the Vienna Albertine Museum. It is reproduced in Gandelman, *Le regard dans le texte,* fig. III.7. See also the *Nude Self-portrait* of 1912 by Schiele reproduced in Erwin Mitsch, *Egon Schiele* (Vienna, 1974), fig. 28, or his *Self-portrait* of 1911, fig. 34.

5. Just as there was a Kubin-Kafka connection, there was a Klee-Kafka connection. Klee and Kafka both published in the Kurt Wolff Verlag, and Klee knew Kubin, whom he calls in his diary "Kubin the benefactor" because Kubin was wont to buy Klee's drawings. Thus, with the three Ks linked in a circle of friendship and benefactorship, there may well have been a contact between Kafka and Klee through the person of Kubin. See Gandelman, "Kafka as Expressionist Draftsman."

6. These insects are of the Phasmida or Phasmitidae family. They are sometimes called walking sticks (Holland) or sticks of the devil (France).

7. Franz Kafka, "A Hunger Artist," trans. Willa and Edwin Muir, in *Short Stories by Franz Kafka* (New York, 1952), pp. 188–189.

8. Ibid., pp. 192–193.

9. Heinrich von Kleist, "Über das Marionettentheater," in *Sämtliche Werke* (Berlin, 1900), pp. 822–828.

10. As noted above (chap. II, n. 19), Brecht implicitly acknowledged his debt to Diderot when he planned to found a Diderot Gesellschaft; this project was never realized.

11. See Marthe Robert, *Seul comme Franz Kafka* (Paris, 1979).

12. Breon Mitchell, "Kafka and the Hunger Artists," in *Kafka and the Contemporary Critical Performance: Centenary Readings,* ed. Alan Udoff (Bloomington, Ind., 1987), pp. 236–255.

13. See ibid., p. 241. The term *hunger artist* was a translation of the Italian *digiunatore,* as explained by the German physiologist M. O. Fraenkel in *Das Hungern: Studien und Experimente am Menschen* (Leipzig, 1890).

14. One such book was *Fisiologia del digiuno: Studi sull'uomo,* by Luigi Luciani (Florence, 1889). It was translated into German by Fraenkel as *Das Hungern.*

15. Mitchell, "Kafka," p. 239.

16. Franz Kafka, *Letters to Milena,* ed. Willi Haas (London, 1953), p. 256.

17. Louis Ginzberg, "How the World Was Created by Means of the Letters," *The Legends of the Jews,* vol. 3 (Philadelphia, 1946), pp. 154–155, and vol. 5, p. 64. An American version of the legend was illustrated by Ben Shahn, *The Alphabet of Creation* (New York, 1965).

18. The consonantal suite YHVH cannot be vocalized. From the Jewish point of view it is an aberration even to try to pronounce it as Yahweh or Jehovah.

19. The Jewish and Islamic draftsmen could always claim that they were merely writing shapes and not drawing them. Drawing with letters is used to subvert the interdiction, but the subversion is perfectly "legal" and therefore legitimate.

20. This may be one source for Derrida's diatribes against logocentrism.

21. These drawings are reproduced in Jürgen Spiller, *The Thinking Eye* (New York, 1959), figs. 341, 122, and 461.

22. Reproduced in Jean (M.), *Histoire de la peinture surréaliste* (Paris, 1959), p. 148.

23. See esp. François Secret, *Les kabbalistes chrétiens de la Renaissance* (Paris, 1964). See also Gerschom G. Scholem, *Kabbalistes chrétiens* (Paris, 1979), and Frances A. Yates, *The Occult Philosophers in the Elizabethan Age* (London, 1980).

24. George Lukács, *Wider den missverstandenen Realismus* (Hamburg, 1958), p. 47.

25. Inscriptions in *Caligari* appear on the city walls repeatedly: "Du musst Caligari werden!" The hero, of course, never "becomes Caligari," and does not even meet Caligari. Indeed, as the end of the story reveals, there is no such man as Caligari.

26. The mystery at the core of *The Thin Man* rests on the fact that the detectives surmise that a man discovered in a cellar was fat, since the clothes found beside the skeleton are those of a person of enormous size. The body had been disintegrated by acid; the victim was actually a thin man.

27. Dashiell Hammett, *The Glass Key* (Knopf, 1931).

28. Ibid., p. 86.

V. Toeing the Line

1. The story was first published in the pro-Bolshevik literary journal *Krasnaya Nov'* (no. 7, 1923): 108–110. When it was included in an anthology entitled *Raskazy* (Stories), the Moscow publisher GIZ expurgated many passages in which the name of Trotsky was mentioned. I based most of my translation of these excerpts on a version that appeared in another anthology published after Stalin's death, *Izbrannoye* (Selected works) (Moscow, 1966), pp. 288–289. But that publication also expurgated the passage at the end in which Trotsky is presented as the true anti-Kerenski hero, the partisan of the "line." Thus I completed the translation by resorting to a French translation of the story.

2. The Trinity bridge separated Petrograd from the city's proletarian suburbs in which the Bolsheviks had a stronghold. Raising the bridge meant ensuring a relative quiet in the city.

3. Here the 1966 Russian edition I have used stops. The lines that follow— indispensable for understanding the aesthetic-political implications of the story— have been omitted, probably because they show Trotsky as the decisive agent in bringing about Kerenski's downfall. It is to be hoped that the original lines will be restored in any new edition of the story. The full version appears in Efraim Sicher's edition of the 1918 Petersburg version, published by Ardis (Ann Arbor, Mich., 1988), pp. 116–118. The Russian text is copyrighted by Ardis.

4. "Linija, bozestvennaya cherta, vlastitelnijtsa myra," or "nizmennaya, kak deijsvitelnost." *Izbrannoye*, p. 289.

5. The first researcher who, to the best of my knowledge, drew attention to the aesthetic content of "Linija i tsvet" was Efraim Sicher of Ben-Gurion University in Israel. He emphasized the Wölfflinian dichotomy rather than the Rieglian one: "The 'line' and 'color' of the title . . . bears a striking resemblance to Wölfflin's distinction [in *Kunstgeschichtliche Grundbegriffe* (Munich, 1915)]. . . . These relate to two manners of seeing: the clear outlining of figures and objects as against the relatively more blurred emphasis on light and color. 'Line' and 'color' may also recall the turn of the century controversy between rival factions of the World of Art group [Mir Iskusstva],

although there is no specific reference to this in the text. The Petersburg school of 'line' headed by Benois emphasized the two dimensional quality of the picture surface and the visual impression of an immediately experienced moment. The Moscow school of 'color,' on the other hand, also emphasized the flatness of the canvas surface but used an all-over, even color, reflecting the symbolist idea of an intangible mysteriousness that represented a deeper reality. . . .'' Sicher, *Style and Structure in the Prose of Isaac Babel* (Columbus, Ohio, 1986), p. 106.

6. The expression *singing morrows* was coined in the 1930s by the French poet and party member Louis Aragon.

7. See Sergei Eisenstein, *Film Form and Film Sense* (New York, 1949), and V. I. Pudovkin, *Film Technique*, trans. Ivor Montagy (London, 1932).

8. K. S. Malevitch, *Essays on Art: 1915–1928*, vol. 1 (Copenhagen, 1968), pp. 24 and 25.

9. Ibid., vol. 2, p. 143.

10. W. Kandinsky, *On the Spiritual in Art* (New York, 1912).

11. *Punkt und Linie zur Fläsche* (Munich, 1926) was vol. 9 in the Bauhaus series edited by Walter Gropius and L. Moholy Nagy.

12. W. Kandinsky, ''Malen'kie stateiki o bol'shim voprosam: O tochke; O linii,'' *Iskusstvo* (1919–1920); an English version appears in *Kandinsky: Complete Writings on Art*, vol. 1, ed. Kenneth C. Lindsay (Boston, 1982), pp. 421–427.

13. Ibid., p. 425.

VI. Homunculus as Map

1. Wilder Penfield and Theodor Rasmussen, *The Cerebral Cortex of Man: A Clinical Study of Localization of Function* (New York, 1968), chap. 2, esp. pp. 24–60, and chap. 11, esp. pp. 210–215. See also Warren Gorman, *Body Image and the Image of the Brain* (St. Louis, 1969), esp. pp. 17–21.

2. See Jakob von Uexkuell, *Niedergeschaute Welten: Die Umwelten meiner Freunde: Ein Erinnerungsbuch* (Berlin, 1936), and ''A Stroll through the Worlds of Animals and Men: A Picture Book of Invisible Worlds,'' in *Instinctive Behavior: The Development of a Modern Concept*, trans. and ed. Claire H. Schiller (New York, 1957). On Von Uexkuell, see Thomas A. Sebeok, *The Play of Musement* (Bloomington, Ind., 1984), pp. 276–277.

3. See Max Black, *Models and Metaphors* (Ithaca, N.Y., 1962).

4. See Frederic Jameson, *The Political Unconscious: Narrative as a Socially Symbolic Act* (Ithaca, N.Y., 1982).

5. Mikhail Bakhtin, *Rabelais and His World*, trans. Helene Iswolsky (Cambridge, Mass., 1968), esp. pp. 26–28.

6. See the diatribe of Bernard of Clairvaux against the ''beautiful monsters and monstrously beautiful sculptures'' of the cathedrals, which also refers to the obscene ''devil-defecating'' monsters sometimes found in Romanesque cathedrals. His letter is in *A Documentary History of Art*, vol. 1, ed. Elizabeth Holt (New York, 1957), p. 27. See also Margaret C. Randall, *Images in the Margins of Gothic Manuscripts* (Berkeley, Calif., 1966).

7. Reproduced in Eduard Fuchs, *Die Karikatur der europäischen Völker* (Munich, 1915), p. 25.

8. Reproduced under the title ''Moloch'' in William Feaver, *Masters of Caricature from Hogarth and Gillray to Scarfe and Levine* (New York, 1981), p. 92.

9. The inventor of phrenology was German: Franz Joseph Gall, the author of *On the Functions of the Brain*, published in the 1820s. But phrenology soon became extremely popular in the English-speaking world. Lectures by the American George

Combe on the subject took place in Boston as early as 1818. A phrenology journal was founded in Edinburgh. In 1834, Combe published his collected essays, *A System of Phrenology*.

10. See J. Lacan, *Ecrits* (Paris, 1966), pp. 89–97.

11. Parmigianino's convex mirror is reproduced in Gustav René Hocke, *Die Welt als Labyrinth: Manier und Manie in der europäishen Kunst* (Hamburg, 1957), pl. I.

12. At the time of the French Revolution, one finds a late version of the representation in *L'Ami du Roi*, the royalist paper. See Jean-Paul Bertaud, *Les amis du roi: Journaux et journalistes en France, de 1789 à 1790* (Paris, 1984), p. 132.

13. The 1839 edition of Hobbes's *Commonwealth* (London) reproduces the original front page of earlier editions. It was also used as the frontispiece of *Representing the English Renaissance*, ed. Stephen Goldblatt (Berkeley, Calif., 1988). On the creation of the front page proper, see K. Brown, "The Artist of the Leviathan Title-Page," *British Library Journal* 4 (no. 1, 1978). Brown thinks Hobbes himself participated in the drawing of the figure.

14. See Claude Gandelman, "Le corps du roi comme carte du royaume," in *Idéologie et propagande en France*, ed. Myriam Yardeni (Paris, 1989), pp. 19–26.

15. Ibid., pp. 22–23.

16. To the best of my knowledge, Imre Herrman's work, originally published in Hungarian, has not been translated into English. I have relied on French translations of two of his works: *Instinct filial* (Paris, 1972) and *Psychologie de l'antisémitisme* (Paris, 1986).

17. Herrman, *Psychologie de l'antisémitisme*, pp. 71–74. One understands from this description that the phenomenon of anti-Semitism, for Herrman, falls within the province of the "epidermic service" within society.

18. Heinrich Himmler, *Discours secrets* (Paris, 1978), p. 204.

VII. Bodies, Maps, Texts

1. Flaubert, *Madame Bovary*, p. 64

2. The *carte du tendre* is reproduced in J. Bédier, P. Hazard, and P. Martin, *Littérature française* (Paris, 1948), p. 333.

3. The first edition of Bunyan's masterpiece, in 1678, was not endowed with a map. It was in 1790 that the cartographer John Wallis published a map, perhaps by his own hand, entitled "Pilgrim's Progress Dissected." This map was reproduced in the catalogue for an exhibition organized by the British Library: *Cartographical Curiosities*, ed. Gillian Hill (London, 1978), fig. 24, p. 22.

4. "Envahis moi comme une armée / Prends mes plaines prends mes collines. . . ." Louis Aragon, "Chanson du miroir déserté," in *Elsa* (Paris, 1959), p. 25.

5. The series is reproduced in *André Masson: Massacre et autres dessins* (Paris, 1971 and 1972).

6. Alechinsky's map pictures are discussed by Michel Butor and Michel Sicard in *Alechinsky dans le texte* (Paris, 1984), pp. 87–88, 129, 130. *Partant du Lac Ch'lin*, 1982, an india ink drawing over an aerial navigator's map, is reproduced in the book, pl. III.

7. See Ginzberg, *Legends of the Jews*, vol. 5, pp. 64, 94.

8. Octavio Paz, *El signo y el garabato* (Mexico City, 1975), pp. 47–48; my translation.

9. See Gandelman, "Le corps du roi," pl. I.

10. The Lérida "world map" is reproduced in Georges de Champeaux and Dom Sebastian Sterckx, *Introduction au monde des symboles* (Paris, 2d ed., 1972), p. 249.

11. Ibid., pp. 249–250.

12. Ernst Kris, *Psychoanalytic Explorations in Art* (New York, 1974), pp. 118–128.

13. Richard Salomon, *Opicinus de Canistris: Weltbild und Bekenntnis eines Avignonesischen Klerikers des 14. Jahrhunderts* (London, 1936).

14. Michel de Certeau, *La fable mystique, XVIe–XVIIe siècles* (Paris, 1982).

15. *John Donne: A Selection of His Poetry*, ed. J. Hayward (London, 1966), p. 177.

16. Ibid., p. 24.

17. Ibid., p. 89.

18. Reproduced in Jacques Bousquet, *La peinture maniériste* (Neuchâtel, 1964), p. 232.

19. *John Donne*, p. 86.

20. Erich Auerbach reproduced the passage and analyzed it at length; see chap. XI, *Mimesis* (Bern, 1946), pp. 250–270.

21. Joseph Roth, *Radetzky Marsch* (Hamburg, 1958), p. 159; my translation.

22. The map is reproduced in *Cartographical Curiosities*, fig. 65, p. 53.

23. Quoted by René Bray, *La préciosité et les précieux* (Paris, 1960), pp. 198–199.

24. Translation by William Aggeler in Charles Baudelaire, *The Flowers of Evil* (Fresno, Calif., 1954), pp. 82–83.

25. Baudelaire's portrait of Hugo was for "Les poètes français," a series of portraits that was never published. See Baudelaire, *Oeuvres complètes* (Paris, 1975), p. 842. Swedenborg was an eighteenth-century representative of the erotic theology of the God-Body.

26. Reproduced in W. Timm, *The Graphic Art of Edvard Munch* (New York, 1972), figs. 47, 31, 75.

27. Joseph Campbell, "Finnegan the Wake," in *James Joyce: Two Decades of Criticism*, ed. Seon Givens (New York, 1948, 1963), p. 368.

28. Joseph Campbell and H. Morton Robinson, *A Skeleton-Key to Finnegans Wake* (New York, 1968), p. 39.

29. James Joyce, *Finnegans Wake* (New York, 1967), p. 7.

30. Ibid., p. 200.

31. Ibid., p. 201.

32. Ibid., p. 208.

33. Reproduced in W. Haftmann, *Nolde* (Cologne, 1974), fig. 4, p. 15.

34. This etching, in my personal collection, was published in *Kunstmappe* (Munich, 1913).

35. Reproduced in Spiller, *The Thinking Eye*, p. 66.

36. Reproduced in *El Lissitski* (Dresden, 1967), fig. 1.

37. Reproduced in J. Barnicot, *A Concise History of Posters* (London, 1972), fig. 248, p. 238.

38. Reproduced in A. H. Barr, Jr., *Fantastic Art, Dada, Surrealism* (New York, 1975), p. 238.

39. See R. Bertelé, *Henri Michaux* (Paris, 1975), pp. 120–121.

40. H. Michaux, *Paix dans les brisements* (Paris, 1959).

41. Juan Luis Borges, *Obras completas* (Buenos Aires, 1974), p. 854.

VIII. The Scatological Homunculus

1. Another revolution, the one in Russia in 1917, produced a passage in Isaac Babel's story "The Goose I Killed" that also draws an analogy between the body and ordnance: "A young fellow, beautiful as only those of Riazan can be, stepped toward my suitcase, which he sent flying in the air through the porch. Thereafter, training his hind parts toward me, he emitted with great skill a series of unmentionable sounds. 'To your ordnance! Number two zero zero: running fire!' shouted one of his

elders, laughing. . . ." This is my own translation from the French edition of Babel's *Kon armia: Cavalerie rouge* (Paris, 1959), p. 88. The French translation is by Maurice Parijanine.

2. These are the years between which Mona Ozouf chose to locate her study, *La fête révolutionnaire: 1789–1799* (Paris, 1978).

3. Albert Boime, "Jacques Louis David, Scatological Discourse in the French Revolution, and the Art of Caricature," *Arts* 62 (no. 6, February 1988): 72–82, covers some of the territory but does not attempt, as I do, to integrate revolutionary caricature into a total system of discourse concerning the body.

4. Jean Starobinski, *L'invention de la liberté* (Geneva, 1970); see esp. "Les emblèmes de la raison." See also Ernst Gombrich, "Nostra signora della libertà," *FMR* (no. 34, June–July 1985): 89–112.

5. There are, of course, exceptions, such as Krafft-Ebbing. His follower Gershon Legman produced a monumental study, *Rationale of the Dirty Joke* (London, 1968). Earlier, the American anthropologist and ex-cavalry officer John G. Bourke published *Scatologic Rites of All Nations* (Washington, D.C., 1891), his doctoral dissertation.

6. "The hunt that was organized without pause during the Restoration against this sort of pictures created enormous gaps. Everything which assaulted the [sexual life] of the Royalty [the police] could lay their hands on, whether in archives, private cabinets and the like, was destroyed without hesitation. The justification for preserving 'historical documents' was ignored by the Restoration. The broadsheets were put under the heading of 'upshoots of subversion' and as it was feared that they would cause a proliferation of horrors of this same type, they were destroyed as soon as they were sighted and in whatever place they were found." Eduard Fuchs, *Das erotische Element in der Karikatur* (Berlin, 1904), p. 183; my translation.

7. The almanac *Etrennes aux fouteurs democrates, aristocrates, impartiaux, ou le calendrier des trois sexes: Almanach lyrique orné de figures analogues au sujet: Sodome et Cythère, à Paris* has the subtitle *Se trouvent plus qu'ailleurs dans la poche de ceux qui les condamnent* (1790, Pet. In–12). See John Grand-Carteret, *Les almanachs français: Bibliographie iconographie* (Paris, 1896), entry 981, p. 253.

8. According to Theme-Becker, *Allgemeiner Lexikon der Bildenden Künstler* (Leipzig, 1928), "Als Denons graphische Hauptwerke nennen wir L'Oeuvre Priapique," 23 Radierungen, Paris 1793.

9. Cited by Ozouf, *La fête révolutionnaire*, p. 104. Almost the same term reappeared after the liberation of France during the Second World War, at the time of the so-called *épuration* of the *collaborateurs;* there was again a public projection of the "body" of France that was supposed to be "purged" of its enemies.

10. Bakhtin, *Rabelais and His World*, p. 119. Bakhtin noted a basic error of the revolutionary spirit: "Guiguené seeks to discover Rabelais' social and political concepts, but using a historicism which is obvious and typical of a man of the eighteenth century. He presents Rabelais as a systematic foe of royal power. In reality, however, Rabelais was never an enemy of this power but on the contrary perfectly understood its progressive meaning at the time."

11. The full title reads "Vanitas vanitatum et omnia vanitas," the famous assertion in Ecclesiastes which was one of the Old Testament foundations on which rested the universal contempt of worldly riches preached by the Roman Catholic Church; it was from this assertion that the genre of the Vanitas originated.

12. Vivan-Denon's first picture album appeared under the name *Voyage pittoresque de Naples et de Sicile par l'Abbé Saint-Non* (Paris, 1788).

13. It seems to have been customary with Jewish artists of the period to draw upon biblical imagery when dealing with the French Revolution, and to represent the

execution of the king and queen in terms of the execution of Haman as described in the Book of Esther. See *Le tournant décisif: Les juifs en France sous la révolution et l'empire* (Tel Aviv, 1981), fig. entitled "Meguilat Esther, en Papier, Alsace, vers 1894. . . ."

14. See Randall, *Images in the Margins of Gothic Manuscripts*, esp. pl. LXXIV, in which hares, the traditional symbols of cowardice, attack a castle and carry on their backs the hunters who dare attack them. See also B. Babcock, *The Reversible World* (Ithaca, N.Y., 1972) and, in it, D. Kunzle, "World Upside-Down: The Iconography of a European Broadsheet Type," pp. 89–94; also Claude Gandelman, "Monde renversé et carré sémiotique," *Neohelicon* 14 (no. 1, pp. 153–175).

15. Reproduced in Ronald Searle, Claude Roy, and Bernard Borneman, *La caricature: Art et manifeste du XVIe siècle à nos jours* (Geneva, 1974), fig. 6, p. 65.

16. Reproduced in Gandelman, "Monde renversé."

17. The classic work on libertinage and the French Revolution is Peter Nagy, *Libertinisme et révolution* (Paris, 1970).

18. Vivan-Denon was an interesting figure in those troubled times. He began his career as a protégé of Madame de Pompadour and finished his life as a protégé of Napoleon. He was also an abbot and a would-be aristocrat who was granted a title of nobility (perhaps thanks to Madame de Pompadour) and called himself De Non. With the beginning of the revolution he became a *défroqué* and swore allegiance to the Republic. But since his property was about to be confiscated by the revolutionary state, he thought of leaving France, probably for England. Due to the protection of David, however, he retained some of his property, renounced his titles, and became a virulent producer of antiroyalist and anticlerical pictures. The etchings presented in this chapter were not his sole scurrilous productions, according to Theme-Becker, *Allgemeiner Lexikon*.

19. Luther's shout is quoted by Erik H. Erikson, *Young Man Luther: A Study in Psychoanalysis and History* (New York, 1958), p. 244. Other references are to pp. 224 and 79.

20. According to Erikson there was first an oral stage in the development of Luther's ideas—the attack against Mother Church—and then an anal-sadistic stage, in which Luther was grappling with the image of the father, that is, of the pope as antichrist or devil. It would not be difficult to transpose Erikson's model to the development of the French Revolution. The prerevolutionary activity at the time of the Diamond Necklace Affair concerned essentially the discrediting of the mother, Marie Antoinette. The second stage was directed against the king and culminated in his beheading.

21. Erikson notes that Luther "had woodcuts made representing the Church as a whore giving rectal birth to a brood of devils"; ibid., p. 246.

22. It is reproduced in Fuchs, *Das erotische Element in der Karikatur*, fig. 66, p. 85.

23. *L'homme machine* was first published in Leiden in 1747. It may be found in an excellent paperback edition published by J.-J. Pauvert in 1966, with an introduction and notes by G. Delaloye.

24. Jean Paul Marat, *De l'homme, ou des principes et des lois de l'influence de l'âme sur le corps et du corps sur l'âme* (Amsterdam, 1775–1776).

25. Quoted by Fuchs, *Das erotische Element in der Karikatur*, p. 182.

26. Quoted by Bertaud, *Les amis du roi*, pp. 98–99.

27. Even such a superb historian of the revolutionary spectacles as Mona Ozouf did not try to escape Freudian influence. She noted the frequent animalization of the figure of the king during specific allegorical fêtes and posed the question (*La fête révolutionnaire*, p. 104): "Freud, qui suggère que les déplacements de la figure de père vers la figure animale est un des thèmes de la névrose infantile conviendrait-il aussi

que l'expression de l'image royale ou papale par la figure animale peut être le thème de la névrose collective?"

28. Sigmund Freud, "Mythologische Parallele zu einer plastischen Zwangsvorstellung," *Gesamm. Werke,* vol. 11, p. 399.

29. *Ostentio,* a term used by Wittgenstein in his *Philosophical Investigations,* stems from Saint Augustine's *Confessions,* I/8, where the saint tells about the way his elders taught him language by pointing toward a thing (*ostendere*).

30. It was, perhaps, the face of God defecating fire and brimstone over Sodom that Lot's wife saw.

31. Georges Bataille, "Histoire de l'oeil," *Oeuvres complètes,* vol. 1, pp. 30–85.

IX. Haptics in Extremis

1. See Frank Whitford, *Kokoschka: A Life* (London, 1986), p. 53, where the architect Adolf Loos tells Kokoschka that he has "X-ray eyes."

2. Edith Hoffman, *Kokoschka: Life and Work* (Boston, 1944), pp. 37, 38.

3. It appeared in the journal *Kunstblatt,* January 1919, p. 17.

4. The *Portrait of the Painter* is reproduced in Hoffman, *Kokoschka,* as pl. XXX. The *Bachkantate,* a series of eleven lithographs illustrating a work by Bach, was published in Berlin by Fritz Gürlitz.

5. See, for instance, Hocke, *Die Welt als Labyrinth;* Arnold Hauser, *Mannerism* (London, 1965); or Jacques Bousquet, *La peinture maniériste* (Neuchâtel, 1964).

6. Charles Estienne's work was written and illustrated between 1530 and 1539 in collaboration with Estienne de la Rivière, a Parisian surgeon. It was published in 1545 in Paris.

7. See Edgard Wind, *Pagan Mysteries in the Renaissance* (New York, 1968), p. 188.

8. La Cava, *Il volto di Michelangelo scoperto nel Giudizio Finale* (Rome, 1925); cited by Wind, *Pagan Mysteries,* p. 188.

9. Michelangelo, *Rime* (Rome, 1889), p. 278.

10. *Poésies de Michel-Ange Buonarroti,* with bilingual text; trans. M. A. Vercollier (Paris, 1826), p. 14.

11. See Anthony Blunt, *Artistic Theory in Italy: 1450–1600* (Oxford, 1962), pp. 72–75.

12. Erwin Panofsky, *Idea: A Concept in Art History* (New York, 1960), esp. pp. 85–93.

13. Walt Whitman, "I Sing the Body Electric," *Leaves of Grass;* see *Walt Whitman* (selected and with notes by Mark Van Doren), in the Viking Portable Library (New York, 1969), p. 129.

14. This Whitmanian theme was echoed in the 1940s in the popular workers' song "Sixteen Tons":

> Some people say a man
> Is made outa mud,
> A man is made
> Outa muscles and blood. . . .

15. See *Walt Whitman,* p. 347.

16. Ibid., pp. 351–352.

17. Ibid., p. 372.

18. Ibid., p. 484.

19. Kafka, *Letters to Milena,* pp. 204–205.

20. The picture is reproduced in Klaus Wagenbach, *Franz Kafka* (Hamburg, 1964), p. 117.

21. Kafka, *Letters to Milena*, p. 256.

22. Thomas Mann, *Der Zauberberg* (Frankfurt am Main, 1966), pp. 385–386; my translation.

23. Ibid., pp. 342–343.

24. Ibid., p. 361.

25. Ibid., p. 259.

26. Ibid., p. 256.

27. Ibid., p. 554.

28. Claude Gandelman, "La pietà de Naphta dans *La montagne magique* de Thomas Mann," *Etudes Germaniques* 32 (April–June 1977), pp. 181–190.

29. Mann, *Der Zauberberg*, p. 545.

30. Antonin Arthaud's concept of a *théâtre de la cruanté*.

31. Thomas Mann, *Doktor Faustus* (Frankfurt am Main, 1966), p. 495.

32. Another possible source for the surrealist severed organ was perhaps the wish to make fun of the neoclassical tradition of the "beautiful antique fragment." Since the Renaissance and above all the baroque period, beautiful classical fragments have figured prominently in Western art. A film such as Cocteau's *Blood of a Poet* may be viewed as a satire of this classical tradition: a classical torso is shown as it undergoes a series of metamorphoses from a wire structure to a snowman and back again. Similarly, iconoclastic tendencies—in the sense of the demolition of the beautiful fragment—seem to pervade Ernst's collages for the *Femme 100 têtes* and *Une semaine de bonté*, where classical fragments, hands and torsos, abound.

33. The fact that the inspiration of both artists stemmed from popular Christian practice and iconography is not without irony when one thinks of Buñuel's virulent anticlericalism.

34. Reproduced in *Salvador Dali: Retrospective* (Musée National d'Art Moderne, Paris), p. 151.

35. Reproduced in *Dali* (Paris, 1968), fig. 26, and in *Salvador Dali: Retrospective*, fig. 243, p. 305.

36. Reproduced in *Salvador Dali: Retrospective*, fig. 244, p. 306.

37. Reproduced in *Retrospective Magritte* (Palais des Beaux-Arts, Brussels, 1978, and Centre National d'Art et de Culture Georges Pompidou, Paris, 1979), fig. 28.

38. Reproduced in W. Chadwick, "Eros or Thanatos: The Surrealist Cult of Love Reexamined," *Art Forum* 14 (November 1975), p. 46.

39. A very clear distinction must be established between two currents. One is antiemotional, cold; it takes pleasure in the anesthetized presentation of the human body in its most bizarre and fantastic aspects. This is the current represented by Vesalius and the tradition of those artists who delight in the theatrical dismemberment of the human body. The second current is that of extreme emotionalism, the expressionist current exemplified by Michelangelo's skin in the Sistine Chapel. German expressionism belongs in the second category.

40. Vladimir Nabokov, *Lolita* (London, 1980), pp. 162–163.

41. From an interview with Peter Beard in *Francis Bacon, Recent Paintings: 1968–1974* (catalogue of the Metropolitan Museum of Art, New York, 1975), pp. 14–15.

42. *Francis Bacon—Recent Paintings, March–April 1967* (Marlborough New London Gallery). Interviews with Francis Bacon by David Sylvester, recorded and filmed in London for BBC-TV, May 1966, p. 35.

43. Interview with Beard, p. 15.

44. Interview with Sylvester, pp. 37, 34.

45. Interview with Beard, p. 15.

46. Salvador Elizondo, *Faraboeuf* (Mexico City, 1965).
47. Ibid., p. 136.
48. Ibid., pp. 135, 139, 145.
49. Ibid., pp. 135–141.
50. Ibid., pp. 140–141.
51. The Museum of Anthropology in Mexico City and the Jalapa Museum in the state of Veracruz display several such statues. The skin around the god is represented by a layer of ceramic scales or is simply carved in stone.

X. Peeling Off Skins

1. See H. W. Janson, "Titian's Laocoön Caricature and the Vesalian Controversy," *Sixteen Studies* (New York, 1973), pp. 39–53.
2. Published in Paris; p. 121. Reprinted in Mittenwald by Maeander Kunstverlag in 1981, after the 1684 Paris edition. The picture seems to have been inspired by baroque renderings of the theme, perhaps by one of the two paintings on the subject by Ribera.
3. Ibid., p. 120.
4. Wind, *Pagan Mysteries*, pp. 172–173.
5. See, for instance, the entry "Allegory" in Richard A. Lanham, *A Handlist of Rhetorical Terms* (Berkeley, Calif., 1969).
6. An allusion to this hermeneutic procedure is doubtlessly present in the title *Marsyas* chosen for their journal by graduate students of the Institute of Fine Arts at New York University.
7. See W. Bacher, *Die Aelteste Terminologie der jüdischen Schriftauslegung* (Leipzig, 1889), p. 25, and Raphael Loewe, "The 'Plain' Meaning of Scripture in Early Jewish Exegesis," in *Papers of the Institute of Jewish Studies London,* vol. 1 (Jerusalem, 1964), pp. 140–186.
8. Ginzberg, *Legends of the Jews,* vol. 5, p. 16 and n. 39. Ginzberg gives as his source *Leben Jesu* by Krauss, esp. the index entry "Grundstein."
9. Here I am adapting Roman Jakobson's concept of the "metalinguistic" function of language.
10. Rudbeck was born in Amsterdam in 1629 and moved to Sweden between 1672 and 1676. He could have been mentioned in chap. VII along with Opicinus de Canistris and Sebastian Münster because he sponsored—or perhaps produced by his own hand—one of the great anthropomorphic maps of all time, a map of the Baltic in the form of Charon. This map is reproduced as fig. 51 in Hill, *Cartographical Curiosities.*
11. *La condition humaine* is reproduced in A. M. Hammacher, *René Magritte* (New York, 1973), pl. 2. *Les promenades d'Euclide* is reproduced in Harry Torczyner, *René Magritte: Signes et images* (Paris, 1977), pl. 473, p. 235.
12. *Le soir qui tombe* is reproduced in Torczyner, *René Magritte.*
13. It is also reproduced in Chastel, *Fables, formes, figures,* vol. 2, p. 221.
14. Reproduced in *American Choice,* ed. William S. Lieberman (New York, 1981), p. 27.
15. Some of Johns's skin paintings are reproduced in Michael Crichton, *Jasper Johns* (New York, 1977), pl. 149 and figs. 86, 87, and 89.
16. See the issue of February 9–15, 1989, pp. 6–7.
17. Arthur Koestler, *Darkness at Noon* (Harmondsworth, 1940), p. 144.
18. I translated this passage from the original Spanish edition, *El hacedor* (Buenos Aires, 1960), p. 103. I kept the capital letters exactly as Borges ordered them in the original.

19. E. T. A. Hoffmann, *Lebens-Ansichten des Katers Murr, nebst fragmentarischer Biographie des Kapellmeisters Johannes Kreisler* (Darmstadt, 1967). Excerpts from this novel may be found in *Selected Writings of E. T. A. Hoffmann*, ed. and trans. J. Kent and Elizabeth C. Knight (Chicago, 1969), pp. 5–99.

20. Géard Genette, *Palimpsestes: La littérature au second degré* (Paris, 1982), esp. pp. 7–19.

XI. Reading Order and Disorder

1. See esp. R. Arnheim, *Entropy and Art* (Berkeley, Calif., 1971); A. M. Bork, "Randomness in the 20th Century," *Antioch Review* 27 (1967), pp. 40–61; Paul G. Kuntz, *The Concept of Order* (Seattle, 1968).

2. E. H. Gombrich, *Art and Illusion: A Study in the Psychology of Pictorial Representation* (Princeton, N.J., 1956), esp. pp. 246–278.

3. I am using this term in its phenomenological—or perhaps Sartrian—acceptation.

4. See. J. A. Schmoll, "Zum Todesbewusstsein in Holbein Bildnissen," *Kunstchronik*, September 1952, pp. 239–242.

5. Indeed, in works devoted to this subject, intentionality is seen as a central element in the definition of the unfinished. See. esp. *Das Unvollendete als künstlerische Form*, ed. J. A. Schmoll (Bern, 1959), and a special issue of the Swiss magazine *Du* on the subject (no. 218, April 1959).

6. See Gerd Schiff's article in the special issue of *Du*, pp. 29-33.

7. See Anthony Blunt, *Artistic Theory in Italy: 1450–1600* (Oxford, 1962), pp. 72–75.

8. One would almost like to speak of three levels: brute language at the everyday level, a first modeling system constituted by newspapers and the other media, and a third modeling system, the work of art.

9. Sterne, *Tristram Shandy*, p. 445.

10. Ibid., p. 6.

11. See Claude Gandelman, "Marcel Proust's Draft Copy-Books: Sketches of His Dreams," *American Imago* (Winter 1977), pp. 297–312.

12. James Joyce, *Finnegans Wake* (London, 1975), p. 185.

13. R. Ingarden, *Das literarische Kunstwerk* (Tübingen, 1965), esp. pp. 261–270.

14. Published in *Konkrete Poesie* (Stuttgart, 1976), p. 23; used by permission of Max Bense.

15. Ibid., p. 142; used by permission of Timm Ulrich.

16. Published in *Text und Kritik* 30 (1965), p. 29; used by permission of *Text und Kritik*, Munich.

17. Published in *Konkrete Poesie*, p. 74; used by permission of H. Heissenbüttel.

18. Max Bense, "Das sogennante 'Anthropische Prinzip' als semiotisches Prinzip in der empirischen Theorienbildung," *Semiosis* 25–26 (nos. 1–2), pp. 13–28.

XII. Oculocentrism and Its Discontents

1. An amusing—or perhaps sad—instance of oculophobia on the part of a "blind" political regime is the story reported in a French paper, *Libération*, about the chief film censor under the Khomeini government in Iran. The man was blind, and the films were narrated to him shot after shot while the narrator and projectionist watched the movements of his hands indicating when cuts had to be made.

2. Michael Kubovy, *The Psychology of Perspective and Renaissance Art* (New York, 1986). Kubovy (p. 11) proves his point by citing a passage from Alberti's *Della Pittura*: "Never let it be supposed that anyone can be a good painter if he does not

clearly understand what he is attempting to do. *He draws the bow in vain who has nowhere to point the arrow"* (Alberti's italics). Kubovy also quotes (p. 14) a passage culled from Filarete's *Treatise on Architecture:* "If you wish to make doors, windows, or stairs, everything should be drawn to this point because, as you have understood, *the centric point is your eye,* on which everything should rest just as the *crossbowman* always takes his aim on a fixed and given point" (my italics).

3. I borrowed the term *oculocentrism* from an unpublished article by Martin Jay, "Scopic Regimes of Modernity."

4. The poster was produced in 1924 by Goskino. It is reproduced in Mildred Constantine and Alan Fern, *Revolutionary Soviet Film Posters* (Baltimore, 1974), p. 45.

5. Reproduced in Stuart Wrede, *The Modern Poster* (New York, 1988), fig. 16, p. 24.

6. Also reproduced in Wrede, *The Modern Poster,* fig. 87, p. 104.

7. Reproduced in Hammacher, *René Magritte,* p. 45.

8. Reproduced as pl. 95 in *Retrospective Magritte.*

9. Shots of this film are reproduced in Lotte Eisener, *The Haunted Screen* (Berkeley, Calif., 1965), p. 220.

10. F. Scott Fitzgerald, *The Great Gatsby* (New York, 1951), p. 183.

11. *Genius* is reproduced in *Max Beckmann,* Catalogue of the Exhibition at the Joseph-Haubrich-Kunsthalle, Cologne, April 19–June 24, 1984, fig. 58, p. 232.

12. Bataille, *Oeuvres complètes,* vol. 1, p. 85.

13. Ibid., p. 38.

14. Ibid., p. 54.

15. Ibid., p. 56.

16. Ibid., p. 69.

17. Ibid., p. 187.

18. Published in 1923. See the American translation by Edwin Honig: Federico García Lorca, *Divan and Other Writings* (New York, Bonewhistle Press, 1972).

19. Ibid., p. 53.

20. Ibid., p. 57.

21. Ibid., n. 1, p. 187.

22. Anthony Burgess, *But Do Blondes Prefer Gentlemen?* (New York, 1986), pp. 5–8.

23. See above, n. 8, chap. I.

24. The anamorphose was discussed in chap. X.

25. Lacan, *Le Séminaire, Livre XI,* pp. 82–83.

26. For Lacan the skull is also paradigmatic of another notion: the idea of the absence/presence of the author. As noted earlier, "hollow skull" is *Hohl-bein* in German and we have here a rebuslike signature of the painter. But it is a signature that signifies absence as well as presence—or perhaps absence more than presence. That is what Lacan terms *décentrement du sujet,* which is to be found in all great works, and especially in all great works of art.

INDEX

CLAUDE GANDELMAN teaches French Literature and Comparative Literature at the University of Haifa, Israel. He is a graduate of the Sorbonne, where he also received his Ph.D. in Comparative Literature. He is co-director of the French-Italian journal *Athanor,* a regular contributor to *Semiotica* and the *American Journal of Semiotics,* and a regular reviewer for the *Yearbook of Comparative Literature* and the *Revue de Littérature Comparée.* His books include *Le regard dans le texte* (Paris, Klincksieck, 1986) and *Littérature et folie* (Paris, Geigy and Synapse Editions, 1989).